THE AMERICAN REVOLUTION

THE AMERICAN REVOLUTION

Other books in this series include:

Ancient Egypt
Ancient Greece
Ancient Rome
The Civil War
The Middle Ages
The Native Americans

THE AMERICAN REVOLUTION

DON NARDO

LUCENT BOOKS®

THOMSON
GALE

San Diego • Detroit • New York • San Francisco • Cleveland • New Haven, Conn. • Waterville, Maine • London • Munich

On cover: *The Attack Upon the Chew House* by Howard Pyle (1853–1911), oil on canvas.

LIBRARY OF CONGRESS CATALOGING-IN-PUBLICATION DATA

Nardo, Don, 1947—
    The American Revolution / by Don Nardo.
        p. cm. — (The history of weapons and warfare)
Summary: Discusses the weapons of Revolutionary War soldiers and different means of warfare used during that conflict.
Includes bibliographical references and index.
    ISBN 1-59018-326-6 (lib : alk. paper)
    1. United States—History—Revolution, 1775-1783—Juvenile literature. 2. Military art and science—United States—History—18th century—Juvenile literature. 3. Military weapons—United States—History—18th century—Juvenile literature. [1. United States—History—Revolution, 1775-1783. 2. Military weapons —History—18th century. 3. Weapons.] I. Title. II. Series.
    E209 .N37 2003
    973.3'3—dc21
                                    2002151095

Printed in the United States of America

Contents

Foreword

The earliest battle about which any detailed information has survived took place in 1274 B.C. at Kadesh, in Syria, when the armies of the Egyptian and Hittite empires clashed. For this reason, modern historians devote a good deal of attention to Kadesh. Yet they know that this battle and the war of which it was a part were not the first fought by the Egyptians and their neighbors. Many other earlier conflicts are mentioned in ancient inscriptions found throughout the Near East and other regions, as from the dawn of recorded history city-states fought one another for political or economic dominance.

Moreover, it is likely that warfare long predated city-states and written records. Some scholars go so far as to suggest that the Cro-Magnons, the direct ancestors of modern humans, wiped out another early human group—the Neanderthals—in a prolonged and fateful conflict in the dim past. Even if this did not happen, it is likely that even the earliest humans engaged in conflicts and battles over territory and other factors. "Warfare is almost as old as man himself," writes renowned military historian John Keegan, "and reaches into the most secret places of the human heart, places where self dissolves rational purpose, where pride reigns, where emotion is paramount, where instinct is king."

Even after humans became "civilized," with cities, writing, and organized religion, the necessity of war was widely accepted. Most people saw it as the most natural means of defending territory, maintaining security, or settling disputes. A character in a dialogue by the fourth-century B.C. Greek thinker Plato declares:

> All men are always at war with one another. . . . For what men in general term peace is only a name; in reality, every city is in a natural state of war with every other, not indeed proclaimed by heralds, but everlasting. . . . No possessions or institutions are of any value to him who is defeated in battle; for all the good things of the conquered pass into the hands of the conquerors.

Considering the thousands of conflicts that have raged across the world since Plato's time, it would seem that war is an inevitable part of the human condition.

War not only remains an ever-present reality, it has also had undeniably crucial and far-reaching effects on human society and its development. As Keegan puts it, "History lessons remind us that the states in which we live . . . have come to us through conflict, often of the most bloodthirsty sort." Indeed, the world's first and oldest nation-state,

Egypt, was born out of a war between the two kingdoms that originally occupied the area; the modern nations of Europe rose from the wreckage of the sweeping barbarian invasions that destroyed the Roman Empire; and the United States was established by a bloody revolution between British colonists and their mother country.

Victory in these and other wars resulted from varying factors. Sometimes the side that possessed overwhelming numbers or the most persistence won; other times superior generalship and strategy played key roles. In many cases, the side with the most advanced and deadly weapons was victorious. In fact, the invention of increasingly lethal and devastating tools of war has largely driven the evolution of warfare, stimulating the development of new counter-weapons, strategies, and battlefield tactics. Among the major advances in ancient times were the composite bow, the war chariot, and the stone castle. Another was the Greek phalanx, a mass of close-packed spearman marching forward as a unit, devastating all before it. In medieval times, the stirrup made it easier for a rider to stay on his horse, increasing the effectiveness of cavalry charges. And a progression of late medieval and modern weapons—including cannons, handguns, rifles, submarines, airplanes, missiles, and the atomic bomb—made warfare deadlier than ever.

Each such technical advance made war more devastating and therefore more feared. And to some degree, people are drawn to and fascinated by what they fear, which accounts for the high level of interest in studies of warfare and the weapons used to wage it. Military historian John Hackett writes:

An inevitable result of the convergence of two tendencies, fear of war and interest in the past, has seen a thirst for more information about the making of war in earlier times, not only in terms of tools, techniques, and methods used in warfare, but also of the people by whom wars are and have been fought and how men have set about the business of preparing for and fighting them.

These themes—the evolution of warfare and weapons and how it has affected various human societies—lie at the core of the books in Lucent's History of Weapons and Warfare series. Each book examines the warfare of a pivotal people or era in detail, exploring the beliefs about and motivations for war at the time, as well as specifics about weapons, strategies, battle formations, infantry, cavalry, sieges, naval tactics, and the lives and experiences of both military leaders and ordinary soldiers. Where possible, descriptions of actual campaigns and battles are provided to illustrate how these various factors came together and decided the fate of a city, a nation, or a people. Frequent quotations by contemporary participants or observers, as well as by noted modern military historians, add depth and authenticity. Each volume features an extensive annotated bibliography to guide those readers interested in further research to the most important and comprehensive works on warfare in the period in question. The series provides students and general readers with a useful means of understanding what is regrettably one of the driving forces of human history—violent human conflict.

How the Patriots Beat the Odds and Won

After the long, steady, and spectacular rise of the United States to the status of the world's sole superpower, it is easy to forget that the success of the rebellion that created the country was by no means a foregone conclusion. In fact, at the time, the odds were decidedly against the American patriots who challenged the British colossus. Though both sides in the American Revolution used roughly the same weapons and battlefield tactics, in most other aspects of warfare the British started out in by far the superior position. Britain was the most powerful empire on earth. The army it sent across the Atlantic was much larger than the meager forces the Americans were able to assemble. By 1781 Britain's troops in North America totaled almost forty-nine thousand, including more than thirty-nine thousand infantry (foot soldiers); American forces, in contrast, were often as low as five thousand men. Moreover, the British troops were better trained, better equipped, and more disciplined than their American opponents.

This American disadvantage was only one of many. The British also had the largest and most feared navy in the world, while the patriots had no navy to speak of. In addition, the Americans started out with fewer muskets and far fewer cannons than the British. And the patriots also had to deal with the hundreds of thousands of colonists who still felt loyal to and sided with Britain in the conflict. These so-called loyalists (whom the British referred to as Tories) not only fought alongside British soldiers but also spied on their neighbors and reported what they saw to the British. It is not surprising, therefore, that a majority of people on both sides viewed the chances of an American victory as slim at best. A respected New York man, Charles Inglis, summed up this view in a popular pamphlet in 1776, warning:

Devastation and ruin must mark the progress of this war. Our seacoasts and ports will be ruined, and our ships taken. Torrents of blood will be spilled and thousands [of people] reduced to beggars.[1]

Exploiting Size, Distance, and Propaganda

Such prophets of doom turned out to be wrong, of course. The patriots possessed and exploited a few advantages of their own, which, combined with some British weaknesses and mistakes, made victory possible in the end. To begin with, the lands the Americans occupied were very large. The strip of territory sandwiched between the Atlantic Ocean and the Appalachian Mountains was several times larger than Britain. Also, the former colonists had access to a vast array of natural resources, including arable land, timber, minerals, and metals. Just as important, the country was so large that the British could not hope to control it completely without a gigantic army of occupation. And maintaining such large forces across the expanse of an ocean was beyond the abilities of any nation at the time.

In fact, even the smaller army that Britain managed to send to North America experienced serious problems that impaired the British war effort. In the words of military historian Ian Hogg:

Almost everything the British soldier ate, wore, rode, or fired had to be transported from Britain by ship. . . . [Britain's] administrative machine was split between . . . [numerous] semi-autonomous agencies . . . all of whom had some vital function which they jealously guarded, and all of whom, to a greater or lesser degree, overlapped the functions and responsibilities of some other agency. All this

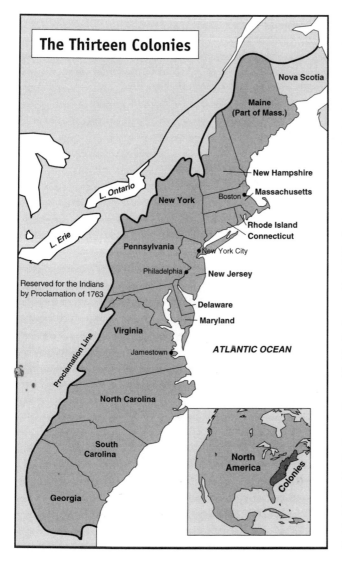

The Thirteen Colonies

ensured a fine climate for rivalry. . . . [The system] proved totally unable to adapt to the needs of the fighting troops, which, in consequence, never managed to produce the results demanded of them.[2]

Just as America's great size and distance from Britain worked to the patriots' advantage, so did the skillful use of propaganda by leading patriots. One of the most effective examples occurred in the hours and days following the war's opening battles, fought at Lexington and Concord on April 19, 1775. These skirmishes, noted historians Henry Commager and Richard Morris point out, were

what the patriots had been waiting for. The British had taken the offensive; the British had fired the first shot. Not only this, but the British had been guilty of atrocities to boot—arson and pillage and rapine and murder. All this the Americans alleged, and doubtless believed [although none of it was true]. We think of propaganda as a modern

Minutemen fire on British troops at Concord Bridge on April 19, 1775. Today a statue of a minuteman stands beside the bridge to commemorate the battle.

development, but there is very little that [we] could teach the patriots of 1775 about propaganda. The Massachusetts Committee of Safety hurried its version [of the events] over to England, and broadcast it throughout the colonies. Never before had news traveled so fast. . . . Everywhere the news of Lexington and Concord strengthened the hands and fired the hearts of the patriots.[3]

Leadership and Fighting Spirit

Another advantage the American rebels possessed was the leadership of a generation of extraordinarily gifted individuals—those who later came to be known as America's founding fathers. In particular, the military and moral leadership of George Washington proved vital to the victory and ultimate survival of the United States. American historian Samuel E. Morison sums up Washington's importance in this eloquent passage:

[Washington] was more than a general. [He was] the embodiment of everything fine in the American character. With no illusions about his own grandeur, no thought of the future except an intense longing to return to Mount Vernon [his Virginia home], he assumed every responsibility thrust upon him, and fulfilled it. He not only had to lead an army but constantly to write letters to Congress, state leaders, and state governments, begging them for the [means] to maintain his army. He had to [mediate] quarrels among his

officers and placate cold, hungry, unpaid troops. . . . Refusing to accept a salary, he dipped into his modest fortune to buy comforts for the soldiers and to help destitute families of his companions in battle. Thus Washington brought something more important to the cause than military ability and statesmanship: the priceless gift of character.[4]

Matching Washington's moral example was the patriotic, often enthusiastic spirit of many American troops, who felt they were fighting for their homes and freedom. No small number of British military officers were aware of this important American advantage. As early as April 1775, a British captain wrote to his father overseas, saying that the rebels, though "the most absolute cowards on the face of the earth," were nonetheless "worked up to such a degree of enthusiasm and madness that they are easily persuaded the Lord is to assist them in whatever they undertake, and that they must be invincible."[5] British general Thomas Gage agreed. "These people show a spirit and conduct against us they never showed against the French [in the recently fought French and Indian War]," he told Britain's secretary of war,

and everybody has judged of them from their former appearance and behavior [i.e., underestimated them] . . . which has led many into great mistakes. They are now spirited up by a rage and enthusiasm as great as ever people were possessed of, and you must proceed in earnest [to send

George Washington's moral and military leadership was a tremendous asset to the Americans. Here, Washington rallies his troops in the Battle of Princeton, in January 1777.

many more troops and supplies] or give the business up.[6]

As it turned out, the British did not pay enough heed to this and other warnings offered by realistic British leaders in both America and England. The Americans' enthusiastic patriotism and desire for free-dom and self-rule, along with their few but crucial other advantages, proved to be decisive factors in their ultimate victory. In the end, it was not superior weapons and battle tactics that allowed the Americans to beat the odds and defeat Britain but, rather, their greater, more stubborn fighting spirit.

CHAPTER ONE

Making and Operating Handheld Guns

Soldiers on both sides in the American Revolution used a fairly wide array of weapons on the battlefield. These included several types of handheld firearms, artillery (cannons), and a variety of bladed weapons (swords, hatchets, spears, and so forth). Of these weapons, the majority of troops relied most on handheld guns, mainly the musket (or firelock), rifle, and pistol. Each of these three broad categories of firearm included a number of different sizes and styles. Although all guns could be lethal if they were handled correctly and the conditions were right, they took a long time to load and were usually not very accurate. For these reasons, the average soldier carried at least one or two other kinds of weapons to use as a backup in case his gun failed him.

In the age in which the American Revolution took place, the musket was the most common firearm carried by foot soldiers. Although the muskets then in use were far from perfect, they were greatly superior to the first version of the weapon,

which had appeared in Europe in the mid-to-late 1300s. The earliest muskets were so long and heavy that they had to be held up by a pole or wooden framework and usually required two men to operate. The 1400s witnessed the invention of smaller versions that could be carried and fired by a single soldier. However, the guns were very inaccurate and took so long to load that a soldier was rarely able to fire more than ten or twelve shots per hour.

Improved Firing Mechanisms

What was needed to improve the performance of early muskets was a more effective and reliable firing mechanism. The existing mechanism consisted of a piece of smoldering rope, called the "match," which the gunman lit, blew on, and then touched to a hole in the barrel, igniting the gunpowder inside. Sometimes the match was wet, which made lighting it impossible; other times, the flame failed to ignite the powder, or if there was too much powder, the weapon misfired or blew up.

At least some of these problems were alleviated with the appearance of the matchlock mechanism in the mid-to-late 1400s. This new firing device consisted of a metal lever bolted to the top of the barrel to hold the smoldering match in place. When the gunner pulled the trigger, a spring snapped the lever back so that the match touched and ignited a small amount of powder in a tiny pan. The flash then penetrated a hole in the barrel, igniting the powder inside and firing the gun.

The matchlock underwent a number of improvements over the years, but the next major technical innovation in musketry

A woodcut depicts a European musketeer in about 1640. He carries his heavy matchlock musket over his shoulder.

did not occur until the mid-to-late 1600s. This was the flintlock. The flintlock ignited the powder in its pan with sparks from a piece of flint hitting against steel, which increased both the reliability and loading speed of the weapon. According to military historian Archer Jones:

The flint, held by the spring-loaded hammer, struck a blow against a plate attached to the cover of the pan, opening the pan as it simultaneously caused sparks which ignited the powder and fired the musket. The mechanism proved much more reliable than the matchlock, initially firing two-thirds of the time as against the matchlock's 50 percent rate. Subsequent improvements enabled the musket to fire 85 percent of the time. The flintlock greatly increased the rate of fire, a process speeded up by the use of an oblong paper cartridge that contained the ball and the proper amount of powder. . . . The musketeer bit off the end of the cartridge with his teeth, retaining the ball in his mouth; used some powder from the cartridge to fill the pan and poured the remainder down the barrel, following it with the ball from his mouth and the paper of the cartridge; he then used his ramrod to drive the paper and ball down on the powder, and he was ready to fire. . . . The soldier with a flintlock with paper cartridge could fire two or three or even more rounds in a minute.[7]

A modern reenactor cocks the firing mechanism of a flintlock musket. The flintlock could be loaded easier and faster than a matchlock, thus increasing the rate of fire.

The flintlock's simpler loading process had the residual effect of changing the composition of infantry formations. Before, two musketeers required at least a yard between them to load properly. By contrast, the easier-loading flintlock required as little as twenty-two inches between men, so a general could double the number of soldiers in each rank (line) on the battlefield. In turn, this increased the firepower of each rank. Still another improvement in the flintlock was the use of stronger metal alloys for the barrel. This allowed for larger, more powerful powder charges, which increased the velocity of a one-ounce musket ball to about one thousand feet per second, making it more lethal than slower-moving balls.

The Muskets of the 1700s

In the 1690s European manufacturers began to turn out flintlock muskets in quantity, and the British and French standardized their own military versions in the early 1700s. At that time the standard British military firearm was the Long Land Service Musket, more commonly known as the "Brown Bess." It weighed about eleven pounds, and its barrel was forty-six inches long. The weapon fired a ball weighing a little over an ounce to an effective range of about two hundred yards. In the mid-1760s the Short Land Service Musket, also referred to as the Brown Bess, appeared, with a barrel thirty-nine to forty inches in length. Better balanced than the Long Land version, the Short Land musket at first supplemented and, over time, slowly replaced the Long Land. Therefore, British soldiers were armed with both versions during the Revolution.

The Brown Bess and the slightly lighter (at just under ten pounds) standard French service musket were also commonly used by Americans in the mid-1700s. Somewhat less common in America were a Prussian (German) musket with a forty-three-inch barrel and a Dutch musket. Much more prevalent, however, were non-standardized muskets made in limited numbers in small American and European workshops; these came in a wide variety of lengths, weights, styles, bores, and calibers (the bore meaning the diameter of the inside of the barrel, and the caliber the expression of the bore in some decimal fraction of an inch). This bewildering diversity of muskets presented no difficulty in peacetime. "It mattered little to a New England farmer," Ian Hogg points out,

if his musket happened to have a bore of .63 [inch] or .72, or some other odd caliber, governed entirely by the boring bit that happened to be handy when the gunsmith made the weapon. The farmer made his own bullets in a mold provided by the same gunsmith, and his expenditure [use] of ammunition was negligible compared to his ability to mold more during his non-hunting periods.[8]

These three models of musket were among the most commonly used in the American Revolution. The top one is a "Brown Bess," and below it is a .69 caliber French service musket.

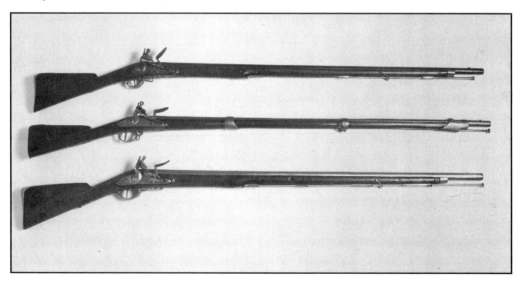

CONGRESS CALLS FOR STANDARDIZING AMERICAN MUSKETS

In July 1775 Congress ordered the committees of safety in the various states to oversee the manufacture of standardized muskets. The following is an excerpt from the congressional resolution (quoted in Harold Peterson's book on colonial arms and armor).

It [is] recommended to the Colonies that they set and keep their gunsmiths at work to manufacture good firelocks with bayonets. Each firelock [is] to be made with a good bridle lock, of ¾ inch bore and of good substance to the breech. The barrel [is] to be 3 feet 8 inches in length, the bayonet to be 18 inches in the blade, with a steel ramrod . . . the price to be fixed by the Assembly or Convention [i.e., Congress] or Committee of Safety of each Colony.

Thus, when American militiamen left their farms and businesses to fight, they carried a wide variety or muskets of varying design and effectiveness. This situation was adequate for a few impromptu battles, but it was decidedly inadequate for fighting a prolonged war, which required arming large numbers of disciplined soldiers with reliable, effective weapons that used standard ammunition. To this end, in July 1775 the infant U.S. Congress called for the manufacture of standardized muskets to be overseen by the various committees of safety, groups set up in the colonies to implement defensive measures.

The result was the American service musket. At first, it was similar to the British Brown Bess, with a barrel length of forty-four inches (halfway between the Long Land and Short Land versions). Eventually, however, the committees of safety adopted a musket closer in design to the lighter French version.

Training and Drilling with Firearms

It was one thing to supply the soldiers of one's army with muskets and quite another to make sure that the weapons were used proficiently and effectively. Firing a flintlock required a series of precise steps executed in a specific order; if the gunman made a mistake in any single step, the weapon failed to fire. And too many such misfires on the battlefield could spell defeat for an army. Consequently, the British carefully and thoroughly drilled their musketeers in the actions of carrying, shouldering, loading, aiming, firing, and reloading their weapons. During training, and often on the battlefield, too, a junior officer in charge of an infantry unit issued a verbal command for each action. This brief excerpt from an official British war manual, *Exercise of the Firelock*, illustrates the extraordinary degree of complexity and precision involved in each action:

A MANUAL EXPLAINS THE PROPER USE OF A MUSKET

This tract is taken from an eighteenth-century British war manual called Exercise of the Firelock *(quoted in Ian Hogg's* Armies of the American Revolution*). It illustrates the large number of individual steps required to operate a musket of that time effectively.*

Upon the command "Prime and Load," make a quarter face to the right . . . at the same time bringing down the firelock to the priming position, with the left hand at the well, the side-brass touching the right hip, the thumb of the right hand placed in front of the hammer with the fingers clenched the firelock nearly horizontal. Open the pan. . . . Upon the command "Handle Cartridge," 1st, draw the cartridge from the pouch. 2nd, bring it to the mouth, holding [it] between the forefinger and thumb, and bite off the top of the cartridge. On the command "Prime," 1st, shake out some powder into the pan and place the three last fingers on the hammer. 2nd, shut the pan. . . . 3rd, seize the small [part] of the butt with the above three fingers. Upon the command "About," turn the piece nimbly round to the loading position, meeting the muzzle [front] with the heel of the hand, the butt within two inches of the ground, and the flat of it against the left ankle. 2nd, place the butt on the ground without noise, raise the elbow square with the shoulder, shake the powder into the barrel [of the musket], putting in after it the paper and ball. 3rd, drop the right elbow close to the body and seize the head of the ramrod. . . . Upon the command "Draw Ramrods," 1st, force the ramrod half[way] out and seize it back-handed exactly in the middle. . . . 2nd, draw it entirely out . . . [and] turning it at the same time to the front, put it one inch into the barrel. Upon the command "Ram Down Cartridge," 1st, push the ramrod down till the second finger touches the muzzle. Second, press the ramrod lightly towards you and slip the two fingers and thumb to the point, then grasp [it] as before. 3rd, push the cartridge well down to the bottom. 4th, strike it two very quick strokes with the ramrod.

An illustration from an eighteenth-century military manual.

Upon the command "Handle Cartridge," 1st, draw the cartridge from the pouch. 2nd, bring it to the mouth, holding [it] between the forefinger and thumb, and bite off the top of the cartridge. On the command "Prime," 1st, shake out some powder into the pan and place the three last fingers on the hammer. 2nd, shut the pan. . . . 3rd, seize the small [part] of the butt with the above three fingers. Upon the command "About," turn the piece nimbly round to the loading position, meeting the muzzle [front] with the heel of the hand, the butt within two inches of the ground, and the flat of it against the left ankle.[9]

This and similar manuals go on and on in the same manner, providing exact instructions for each command. The chain of steps involved may seem overly complicated to the modern observer who is accustomed to the more simple operation of modern guns. However, through repeated drills and practice, eighteenth-century British soldiers became so adept that their performance was fluid and almost automatic.

At first, most of the musketeers of the American regular army lacked this kind of precise instruction and the formal drilling that accompanied it. This deficiency contributed to the several defeats the patriots suffered in the early stages of the war. In 1778, however, General Washington charged an experienced Prussian soldier—Baron Frederick von Steuben—with the task of instituting systematic musket training and drills. Steuben trained the Americans in European, or "Continental," methods and tactics and subsequently issued a manual that remained standard in the U.S. Army well into the nineteenth century. This excerpt covers the actions of cocking and aiming a flintlock musket:

> [To cock the firelock,] turn the barrel opposite to your face, and place your thumb upon the cock, raising the elbow square at this motion. Cock the firelock by drawing down your elbow, immediately placing your thumb upon the breech-pin, and the fingers under the guard. [To aim the firelock,] step back about six inches with the right foot, bringing the left toe to the front; at the same time drop the muzzle and bring up the butt-end of the firelock against your right shoulder; place the left hand forward on the swell of the stock, and the forefinger of the right hand before the trigger, sinking the muzzle a little below level, and with the right eye looking along the barrel.[10]

The Introduction of the Rifle

Although the musket could be quite effective if operated correctly, it possessed a serious drawback stemming from the nature of its bore. The inside walls of the barrel were as smooth as a pipe, hence the common term smoothbore musket. For various reasons, including the ease of ramming the lead ball down the barrel, the ball was smaller than the bore. For example, the Long Land Service Musket had a caliber of .753 inch, but the ball it fired was .70 inch in diameter. The space between the edge of the ball and the

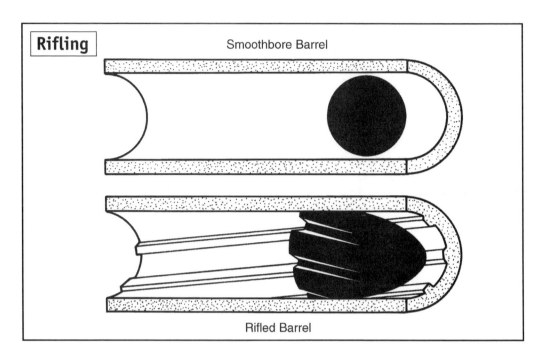

Rifling

Smoothbore Barrel

Rifled Barrel

inside of the barrel, in this case .053 inch, is called windage. The problem was that windage allowed the ball to wobble from side to side as it moved down the barrel, so it exited the gun slightly off center, contributing to its inaccuracy. To make up for the lack of accuracy of individual muskets, the guns usually were fired in large numbers simultaneously. That way at least some of the shots were likely to hit the enemy.

In contrast, another firearm used in the Revolution—the rifle—largely eliminated this drawback. The term rifle is derived from the weapon's "rifling," or set of spiral grooves etched into the inside walls of the barrel. When the weapon fired, the ball spun through the grooves and exited the gun spinning; at the same time, the ball made a tight fit in the bore, almost eliminating the windage. The result was a much

more accurate shot. Another advantage of the rifle, Hogg explains, was its

> greater range and velocity, due again to the tight fit of the ball. The musket ball's windage allowed a proportion of the propelling gas to rush past and be wasted in muzzle blast, whereas the rifle ball, firmly lodged in the rifling, sealed all the gas behind it and extracted every available scrap of performance from the powder.[11]

No one knows for sure when the concept of rifling a gun was first introduced. Early specimens dating from the 1540s have survived. However, the manufacturing technique required special tools and much skill, so the rifle was not widely adopted until the 1600s, and even then it remained mainly a hunter's weapon. The rifle reached the American colonies in the early 1700s when German and Swiss gunsmiths emigrated across the Atlantic and set up shop. At first, they produced large weapons with calibers ranging from .50 to .70 inch, but over time American fron-

tiersmen demanded lighter guns with smaller bores, so a more distinctly American version with a bore of .45 inch became common. Because most of the gunsmiths who made this version lived in Pennsylvania's Lancaster County, it became known

A SNIPER TAKES DEADLY AIM

George Hanger, a British officer who was captured by the Americans at Saratoga and survived the war, later penned this compelling eyewitness account (from his book Colonel George Hanger to All Sportsmen) *describing the amazing skill of an American rifleman.*

Colonel Tarleton, and myself, were standing a few yards out of a wood, observing the situation of a part of the enemy which we intended to attack. . . . It was absolutely a plain field between us and mill; not so much as a single bush on it. Our orderly-bugler stood behind us about three yards. . . . A[n American] rifleman passed over the mill-dam, evidently observing two officers, and laid himself down on his belly; for in such positions, they always lie, to take a good shot at a long distance. He took a deliberate and cool shot at my friend, at me, and at the bugle-horn man. Now observe how well this fellow shot. It was in the month of August, and not a breath of wind was stirring. Colonel Tarleton's horse and mine, I am certain, were not anything like two feet apart. . . . A rifle-ball passed between him and me; looking directly to the mill I . . . observed the flash of the powder. I directly said to my friend, "I

think we had better move." . . . The words were hardly out of my mouth when the bugle-horn man behind me . . . jumped off his horse and said, "Sir, my horse is shot." The horse staggered, fell down, and died. . . . Now speaking of this rifleman's shooting, nothing could be better. . . . I have passed several times over this ground and ever observed it with the greatest attention; and I can positively assert that the distance he fired from at us was [a] full 400 yards!

One of Daniel Morgan's famous riflemen prepares to fire his weapon.

as the "Pennsylvania rifle." (The romantic but less accurate term Kentucky rifle, better known today, was not applied to the weapon until the early nineteenth century.)

The rifle remained only a supplement to the less-accurate musket in the American Revolution however, mainly because the rifle took much longer to load. The rifleman first had to force the ball into the rifling near the muzzle, often with a mallet, and then use his ramrod to push it farther down the barrel. Most riflemen could get off only one shot per minute, or two at best. That was enough time for an enemy soldier to close in and bayonet the rifleman before he was finished reloading. Therefore, the rifle was largely impractical in large battles. In fact, American general Anthony Wayne wrote to a colleague that he "would almost as soon face an enemy with a good musket and bayonet without ammunition,"[12] as with a rifle.

Rifles in the Hands of Expert Marksmen

Despite the fact that rifles took so long to load, an expert marksman armed with a rifle could pick off individual enemy soldiers, especially officers, at surprisingly long range. In a battle fought at Bemis Heights, New York, in September 1777, a famous squad of riflemen under Daniel Morgan successfully killed several English officers at long range. After the battle, the defeated British commander, General John Burgoyne, recalled:

The enemy had with their army great numbers of marksmen, armed with rifle-barrel pieces [i.e., rifles]. These, during the engagement, hovered upon the flanks [sides] in small detachments, and were very expert in securing themselves and in shifting their ground. In this action, many placed themselves in high trees in the rear of their own line, and there was seldom a minute's interval of smoke in any part of our line without officers being taken [picked] off by single shots.[13]

Another British officer, George Hanger, whom the Americans took prisoner about a month later at Saratoga, New York, had a chance to meet some of these notorious sharpshooters. He later wrote:

I have many times asked the American backwoodsmen what was the most their best marksmen could do. They have constantly told me that an expert rifleman, provided he can draw good and true sight . . . can hit the head of a man at 200 yards. I am certain that provided an American rifleman was to get a perfect aim at 300 yards at me standing still, he most undoubtedly would hit me, unless it was a very windy day.[14]

Fortunately for Hanger, he was never hit by an American rifleman. The fate of one British officer who *was* so hit turned out to be one of the great ironies of the war. Long a gun enthusiast as well as a soldier, Scotsman Patrick Ferguson invented his own version of the rifle, which modern experts believe was the most effective firearm made in the eighteenth century. Reportedly, it could fire four to six shots per minute, making it faster, as well as more accurate, than any musket. In April 1776 Ferguson demonstrated his rifle to his superiors, who were impressed enough to have him make one hundred more. To test the new weapon, in September 1777 Ferguson led a unit of a hundred British riflemen into battle at Brandywine Creek in Pennsylvania. Unfortunately, he was seriously wounded before his men could prove themselves and the British unwisely disbanded the unit. If they had instead replaced all their muskets with Ferguson rifles, they might well have won the war. (The fate of all but one of these prototypes of Ferguson's remarkable rifle is unknown. The single surviving weapon, found years later in a New England attic, now rests in the museum at Morristown National Historic Park in New Jersey.)

Ferguson recovered from his wound and fought the Americans again. In October 1780 at King's Mountain, near the border of North and South Carolina, the great rifleman was done in by swarms of

Most American muskets used in the war were made by hand. Here, gunsmiths in a local shop forge the barrels and assemble the firing mechanisms.

his American counterparts. One of them, James Collins, later recalled:

> On examining [Ferguson's body] . . . it appeared that almost fifty rifles must have been leveled at him at the same time. Seven rifle balls had passed through his body, both his arms were broken, and his hat and clothing were literally shot to pieces.[15]

Fighting with Pistols

While the design and quality of flintlock muskets were improving, a parallel development was taking place with flintlock pistols. To load and fire such a pistol required the same precise and laborious series of steps involved in the use of other flintlock weapons. And similarly, rifled pistols were more accurate than smoothbore versions. Although most were muzzle loaded, some pistols had barrels that unscrewed, allowing them to be breech loaded (i.e., loaded from

This brass flintlock pistol is equipped with a spring bayonet (seated below the barrel).

the back end), which eliminated the need for a ramrod. Being smaller, the typical pistol naturally lacked the firepower of a musket or rifle; to compensate somewhat, some gunsmiths made versions of pistols with double barrels.

The gunsmiths who made the British and American pistols used in the American Revolution employed a diverse range of craftsmen. As explained by military historian Warren Moore:

> The tradesmen involved in the fabrication of pistols consisted of a barrelforger, locksmith, wood stocker or carver, engraver, and metalsmith. Almost all English pistols had the maker's name engraved or stamped across the lockplate, and sometimes on the barrel also. Some of the later firms made the entire gun in their shops, employing workers from all of the trades mentioned above. Others were simply assemblers of parts which were made to their specifications by the respective specialists, the finished product being assembled by workers in their shops.[16]

In peacetime, most pistols manufactured before the mid-nineteenth century were used for individual self-defense, protecting one's home, or dueling. In wartime, most infantrymen did not carry pistols, partly because it was too difficult for a foot soldier to carry and use both pistols and muskets and also because belt holsters had not yet been invented. The use of the weapon was limited mainly to officers, who customarily did not carry muskets or rifles; sailors, who used pistols in the hand-to-hand combat

TEACHING ONE'S HORSE NOT TO FEAR GUNFIRE

Unlike infantry officers and sailors who wielded pistols, cavalrymen had to worry about the discharge these weapons produced frightening their horses. A 1778 military manual, The Discipline of the Light Horse (quoted in Warren Moore's volume on weapons of the American Revolution), gave the following advice about acclimating a horse to the sound and smell of its rider's pistol.

To [get your] horse [used] to [the discharge of] fire arms, first put a pistol . . . in . . . with his feed, [get him used] to the sound of the lock and pan [i.e., cocking the weapon]; after which, when you are upon him, show it [the pistol] to him, presenting it forwards, sometimes on one side, sometimes on the other; when he is reconciled to that, proceed to flash in the pan [ignite the powder]; after which, put a small charge into the piece, and so continue augmenting it [increasing the size of the charge] by degrees. . . . If he seems uneasy, walk him forwards a few steps slowly, and then stop, [move him] back, and caress him.

that occurred when they boarded enemy ships; and cavalrymen, who found a pistol easier to wield than a musket or rifle while charging on horseback.

In the opening years of the war, American cavalrymen and sailors used mainly British-made pistols, which at the time were the most common version in the former colonies. As time went on, however, pistols were imported from numerous foreign countries. The most popular were Dutch models, which featured calibers ranging from .65 to .69 inch and barrels eleven to fifteen inches long, with a weight of just over three pounds. French versions, which came in a wide variety of designs and sizes, were also popular. The most common pistol used by Americans in the later years of the war was a French version with a caliber of .65 inch, a nine-inch barrel, and a weight of roughly two and a half pounds. Thus, the pistols of the American Revolution were a mix of weapons made in many countries.

CHAPTER TWO

Many Traditional Bladed Weapons

Although firearms such as the musket and rifle saw widespread use in the American Revolution, in that era guns had not yet largely replaced bladed weapons in battle. The simplest general definition for bladed (or edged) weapons describes those having exposed, sharpened metal surfaces useful for stabbing, hacking, and/or cutting an opponent. The main bladed weapons used in America's war for independence were the bayonet, the sword and dagger, the halberd (or poleax), the spear (or pike or spontoon), and the hatchet (a one-handed ax, also called a tomahawk). Some of these weapons were just as prominent on the battlefield as guns were in the American Revolution.

Of all the bladed weapons employed in the war, the bayonet was by far the most common and important. In fact, more than any other single weapon, including the musket, the bayonet determined the winners of most infantry battles in the eighteenth century. Large-scale battles of the American Revolution usually featured long lines of soldiers facing off with bayonets attached to their muskets. After firing their muskets one or more times in a gradual advance, the troops charged the enemy and tried to stab them with their bayonets. At this point, in the face of this onslaught of sharpened metal, it was not unusual for the soldiers of one side to lose their nerve and retreat.

How Bayonets Developed

Such formal bayonet charges were the final development in the steady evolution of shapes and uses of bladed weapons stretching back through many centuries. The bayonet was, in effect, a later version of the pike, a long spear used by infantry soldiers in ancient and medieval times. In the 1300s and 1400s, a few armies, notably the Swiss army, developed large infantry formations of soldiers bearing outstretched pikes. Such a forest of bristling spearpoints proved a formidable defensive barrier on the battlefield, and it was extremely lethal when it marched forward on the offensive. Later, in the 1500s

Long pikes, from which bayonets developed, stand out in this medieval battlescene. The bayonet was essentially the front end of a pike mounted on a musket.

and 1600s, generals combined units of musketeers with their pikemen. The musketeers, whose guns were still very slow to load and therefore vulnerable to enemy infantry and especially cavalry, stood inside a protective barrier of pikes. The pikemen kept the enemy at bay while the gunmen reloaded.

When faster-loading, more reliable flintlock muskets appeared in the 1600s, guns became much more effective on the battlefield. But they were still not reliable or lethal enough to stop a large cavalry charge by themselves. Rows of pikes were still needed for that. A few military innovators recognized that the best solution was to somehow combine both weapons

into one. The result was the introduction of the bayonet, a bladed weapon that simulated the end of a pike and also could be mounted on a musket.

The exact origins of the bayonet are unclear. But the first version used in warfare, called a plug bayonet, was apparently made in France in the mid-1600s. It was essentially a long dagger with a tapering handle; the term plug referred to the fact that the soldier stuffed the handle into the muzzle of his musket, plugging it. In this way, he converted his gun into a pikelike weapon. This allowed a general to convert his pikemen into musketeers, increasing the firepower of his army, while maintaining a way

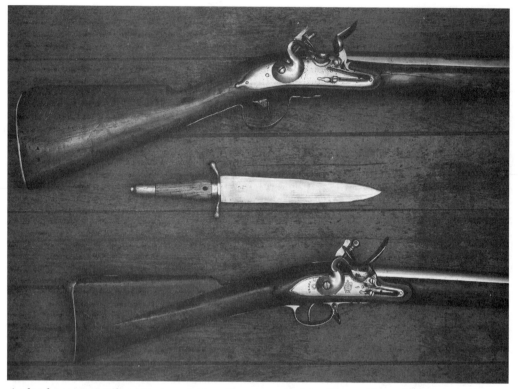

A plug bayonet rests between two eighteenth-century muskets. The problem with this type of bayonet was that the plug had to be removed before the gun could be fired.

to stop cavalry charges. When enemy cavalry threatened, the gunmen fired off a round and then quickly inserted their bayonets, creating a wall of steel to fend off the horsemen.

It soon became clear, however, that plug bayonets created a serious disadvantage. A musket fitted with a plug bayonet could not be fired. So, a soldier could alternately be a gunman or a quasi-pikeman, but he could not be both at the same time. What was needed was a bayonet that could be permanently attached to a musket while leaving the barrel free for firing. That need was filled when the socket bayonet appeared, again in France, in the late 1600s. According to noted military historian George C. Neumann, the socket bayonet featured "a metal sleeve that slipped over the muzzle of the gun":

A narrow neck branching out from the sleeve's upper end supported the blade. Since the blade was now offset from the bore and parallel to the barrel, the musket could be loaded and fired while the bayonet remained in place. Versions of the new socket design were widely adopted by both the English and French armies just after 1700—although the "plug" continued in use for at least another decade.[17]

The Bayonet Crosses the Ocean

By the early 1700s, the bayonet had become one of the two major infantry weapons used in Europe. (The other was the musket itself.) In Britain's American colonies, however, bayonets had not achieved the same popularity. This was probably because most of the fighting the colonists had engaged in over the years had consisted of informal skirmishes against Indians, in which bayonets were of little or no use.

The Americans had their first major exposure to bayonets in the French and Indian War, fought in North America between 1754 and 1763. But most of the fighting was between trained British and French troops, and few colonists gained any real experience with the weapon. For these reasons, at the outset of their war for independence the Americans lacked both appreciation for and skill with what was at the time the most reliable weapon in the British arsenal.

SNEAK ATTACKS WITH BAYONETS

Bayonets were deadly not only on the open battlefield but also in surprise attacks. The so-called Paoli Massacre was a prime example. In mid-September 1777, George Washington sent General Anthony Wayne with a small force to attack the British from the rear. Unfortunately, the British discovered Wayne's camp at Paoli, near Philadelphia, and just after midnight on September 21, British redcoats fell on the camp. Their muskets unloaded, they used only bayonets. The unprepared American soldiers suffered heavy casualties, as reported a few days later by an American major, Samuel Hay (quoted in volume one of Commager and Morris's Spirit of 'Seventy-Six*).*

[It was] a scene of butchery. All was confusion. . . . I need not go on to give the particulars, but the enemy rushed on with fixed bayonets and made the use of them they intended. So you may figure to yourself what followed. The party lost 300 privates in killed, wounded, and missing, besides commissioned and non-commissioned officers. . . . The 22nd, I went to the ground to see the wounded. The scene was shocking—the poor men groaning under their wounds, which were all by stabs of bayonets and cuts of . . . swords. Col. Grier was wounded in the side by a bayonet, superficially slanting to the breast bone. Captain Wilson's stabbed in the side. . . . Andrew Irvine was run through the fleshy part of the thigh with a bayonet.

A modern reenactor affixes a bayonet to his authentic musket.

This shortcoming was not lost on American war planners. In 1775 Congress recommended that each state ensure that its militia had supplies of bayonets. The regular army, commanded by George Washington, needed bayonets even more, since these troops would bear the brunt of the fighting with the highly trained British regulars. There was a rush, therefore, to acquire or produce as many bayonets as possible. Some of those used by American soldiers in the war were captured from British troops or arsenals; others were purchased from the French, Germans, and other Europeans; and still others were manufactured in American forges and workshops. At first, the American-made versions were patterned after British models, but as time went on, they increasingly resembled French bayonets.

The Americans manufactured many bayonets and began training troops in their use, but it took a while before American proficiency matched British skill. Perhaps American officers and soldiers did not fully appreciate how devastating these weapons could be until they won a major battle using only bayonets. This significant event occurred on July 15, 1779, when 1,350 American troops commanded by General Anthony Wayne captured the fort at Stony Point, on the west side of the Hudson River in New York. According to the account of another American officer, Nathanael Greene:

The Americans charge into the British ranks at Stony Point, a battle won by bayonets.

> The attack was made about midnight and conducted with great spirit and enterprise, the troops marching up in the face of an exceeding heavy fire with cannon and musketry, without discharging a gun. This is thought to be the perfection of discipline and will forever immortalize Gen. Wayne, as it would do honor to the first general in Europe. . . . The darkness of the night favored the attack and made our loss much less than might have been expected. The whole business was done with fixed bayonets. Our loss in killed and wounded amounted to

A Very Reliable Bayonet

In this excerpt from his informative book Swords and Blades of the American Revolution, *military historian George C. Neumann describes the standard and very reliable English bayonet, which emerged about 1720 and remained more or less unchanged until the early nineteenth century.*

Its total length was just over 21 inches. The 4-inch long socket had an outside diameter of slightly more than one inch, and a rear reinforcing ring. Its blade approximated 17 inches from the tip to the base guard and was triangular in cross section (i.e., for stabbing instead of cutting), with a flat top surface. . . . Across the blade's end (where it joined the neck) was a raised triangular base guard. Standard Brown Bess muskets of the 18th century had a top rectangular bayonet stud. The bayonet socket included a three-step slot through which the stud slid.

---

90 men, including officers—eight only of which were killed. . . . The enemy made little resistance after our people [armed with their bayonets] got into the works; their cry was, "Mercy, mercy, dear, dear Americans!"[18]

British losses totaled 63 killed, 70 or more wounded, and 543 captured. Thereafter, American troops used the bayonet with renewed vigor.

Types and Uses of Swords

Next to the bayonet, the leading bladed weapon used in the American Revolution was the sword. Until the advent of widespread use of the bayonet in the early 1700s, the sword was a standard tool of warfare in Europe, the Near East, and beyond for at least five thousand years. Most often it was used as a backup weapon to supplement the spear, bow and arrow, lance, pike, or some other primary weapon.

By the beginning of the American war for independence, however, many, if not most, British and other European infantrymen no longer carried swords into battle. There was no need to—their bayonets performed roughly the same cutting and stabbing functions. There were some exceptions, including grenadiers (elite infantry units), drummers and fifers, and officers, but by the end of the war, except for certain officers, these military men too had largely stopped carrying swords. In contrast, American infantry were somewhat slower to abandon swords. In the opening year of the war, Congress called for soldiers to carry swords and hatchets in addition to bayonets. And although many ordinary foot soldiers gradually stopped wearing swords during the conflict, American officers were actually required to carry them throughout the war.

The situation was quite different outside the infantry. For the cavalry soldier of this period, the saber, a formidable slashing

A member of a reenactment group, the Brigade of the American Revolution, brandishes a cavalry saber.

sword, was the primary offensive weapon; it was seen as more reliable and lethal than the horseman's other main weapon, the pistol. The superiority of the saber was ably summarized by Epaphras Hoyt, a noted Massachusetts cavalry captain, in his *Treatise on the Military Art*:

It is generally agreed by experienced officers, that firearms are seldom of any great utility to cavalry in an engagement. . . . Numerous examples could be cited from military history to show their inefficiency. It is by the right use of the sword that they [cavalrymen] are to expect victory. This is indisputably the most formidable and useful weapon of cavalry. Nothing decides an engagement sooner than charging briskly with this weapon in hand. By this mode of attack, a body of cavalry will generally rout one that receives it with pistols ready to fire.[19]

Hundreds of different styles and sizes of cavalry swords (as well as other kinds of swords) existed. But the most popular type used by American horse soldiers in the Revolution was a light saber with a curved blade. The blade varied in length from 32.5 to 36.5 inches and was attached to the pommel by a small metal nut. The saber wielded by Epaphras Hoyt himself, which is preserved in Memorial Hall in Deerfield, Massachusetts, is of this type.

Sailors also used swords. The naval version of the weapon came to be called a cutlass in the second half of the eighteenth century. The blade of a cutlass, generally a bit shorter than that of a cavalry saber, was straight or slightly curved and had a cutting edge on one side only. The hilt had an unusually wide guard to protect the hand in the close-in fighting common in naval boarding tactics. The average seaman carried his cutlass naked (without a sheath) by thrusting it through his belt.

Smaller Bladed Weapons

In addition to bayonets and swords, several smaller bladed weapons were widely used in the American Revolution. Most American men carried knives of one type or another both on and off the battlefield, for example. Perhaps most common was the belt knife, which had a single-edged blade designed mainly for cutting. It was most often used as a tool—for skinning game, chopping food, whittling, and so forth—but it could also be used as a weapon to stab or scalp someone. A person carried a belt knife either in a leather sheath that attached to the belt or naked in the belt.

COLD-BLOODED MURDER

Soldiers and sailors usually drew their swords only during battle. However, occasionally these weapons were used to kill unarmed civilians or prisoners in cold blood. Today, many Americans are surprised to learn that such atrocities were perpetrated by both sides during the American Revolution. In this excerpt from his gripping narrative of the Battle of Haw River (quoted in John C. Dann's The Revolution Remembered*), in which American troops defeated a force of loyalists (Tories), American fighter Moses Hall describes such butchery.*

The evening after our battle with the Tories, we having a considerable number of prisoners, I recollect a scene which made a lasting impression upon my mind. I was invited by some of my comrades to go and see some of the prisoners. We went to where six were standing together. Some discussion taking place, I heard some of our men cry out, "Remember Buford" [a reference to an earlier massacre carried out by the Tories], and the prisoners were immediately hewed to pieces with broadswords. At first I bore the scene without any emotion, but upon a moment's reflection, I felt such horror as I never did before nor have since, and, returning to my quarters and throwing myself upon my blanket, I contemplated the cruelties of war until overcome and unmanned by a distressing gloom from which I was not relieved until commencing our march [the] next morning.

Pictured are half-axes, or tomahawks, which most American soldiers carried.

The hatchet, or small, one-handed ax, was a common tool and weapon in colonial America. The terms hatchet, half-ax, belt-ax, and tomahawk (an Indian word) were used more or less interchangeably in the colonies in the eighteenth century. Both settlers and soldiers used hatchets for clearing brush and cutting down small trees. And the hatchet's value as a personal weapon became clear early on. Metal hatchets were particularly valuable to white Europeans in the prosperous Indian trade, for they were superior to traditional stone tomahawks and therefore much in demand among Native Americans. One white trader, Sir William Johnson, estimated that he sold about ten thousand hatchets to Indians in the year 1765 alone.

During the American Revolution, a majority of American fighters carried hatchets. Many in the militia and regular infantry had them, and they were standard backup weapons for riflemen. Some British infantrymen also carried the belt-ax as a backup. Because of the secondary role it played, few descriptions of the hatchet's use in battle have survived, but the following exception vividly shows how lethal it (as well as the knife) could be in a fight. In the summer of 1778, an American, David Welch, who was serving in Vermont, took part in a fight to the death with one of Britain's Indian allies. Happening on two Indians beside a campfire in the woods, Welch crept up on them. He later recalled:

Daggers were slightly bigger knives designed specifically for fighting. Such a weapon usually had a symmetrical tapering blade, averaging six to ten inches in length, with two sharp edges so that it could be used both to slash and to stab. Many American soldiers, especially frontiersmen and militiamen, carried daggers; some of them preferred the dagger to the bayonet in hand-to-hand combat. Some British fighters also carried daggers. Most notable was the dirk, of Scottish origin, with a thin, single-edged blade measuring twelve to seventeen inches long.

I drew my gun and whilst lying thus flat on the ground, I took deliberate aim at one of the Indians and shot him dead. The other Indian instantly sprung upon his feet, seizing his gun, and . . . turned and fired upon me, but his fire missed. . . . He then dropped his gun and came at me with his tomahawk. I encountered him with my empty gun. The first blow which he aimed with his tomahawk I warded off with my gun, and in doing it I was so fortunate as to hook the deadly weapon from him. . . . I was then encouraged and sprung to get the tomahawk, in which effort I succeeded. Whilst I was yet bent in picking up the tomahawk, the Indian, who had drawn his knife, gave me a cut, giving me a deep but short wound upon my right leg. . . . He then aimed a second stroke at me with the same weapon. This blow I warded off with my left hand, in doing which I received a wound between the thumb and forefinger. About the same instant, with the tomahawk I hit him a blow on the head which brought him to the ground, and with another blow after he had fallen I made sure he was beyond doing me any further harm.[20]

Traditional Weapons Die Slowly

Still another broad category of bladed weapons used in the American Revolution was collectively referred to as pole arms. It included the halberd and various types of spears (including the pike and spontoon). The halberd, or poleax, was essentially a long spear with an axlike blade mounted near the end. It was commonly used on battlefields in late medieval times across most of Europe, and its metal blades came in a bewildering variety of decorative shapes. An infantryman could use the spearpoint of his halberd to jab at and penetrate an enemy's armor, or he could swing the weapon with two hands like a giant ax. Not surprisingly, one well-placed stroke of this weapon could bring down a horse and its rider.

By the mid-to-late 1600s, with the development of massed units of musketeers, followed by the emergence of the bayonet, the halberd became more or less obsolete as a weapon. However, history has shown that traditional military weapons tend to die very slowly. Soldiers in Europe and America retained the halberd for another century or so, mainly as a symbol of rank. Usually, a sergeant carried it, although soldiers and officials of other ranks did so, too, on ceremonial occasions. The fact that many halberds of the American Revolution had finely sharpened blades indicates that they were still used in battle, though probably only rarely.

As for pikes, the very long versions wielded by the Swiss in late medieval times were replaced by the line of musket-bayonet men that emerged in the late 1600s and early 1700s. However, a shorter pike, or big spear—the spontoon (or espontoon)—survived as a standard tool of warfare in Europe and America. Mostly it was an infantry officer's weapon. British and American officers did not ordinarily carry muskets or rifles on the battlefield. The rationale was that the complicated actions of loading and firing would divert their attention too much from observing the battle and giving orders. So, officers carried spontoons, which became their symbol. George Washington later explained why he felt the spear was essential for an American officer:

> As the proper arming of officers would add considerable strength to the Army, and the officers themselves derive great confidence from being armed in the time of action, the General orders everyone of them to provide himself with a half pike or spear as soon as possible—firearms, when made use of, withdrawing their attention too much from their men, and to be without either, has a very awkward and unofficer-like appearance.[21]

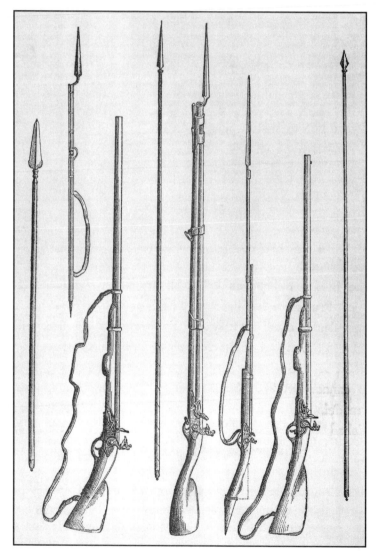

This eighteenth-century drawing depicts common weapons of the period, including spontoons.

Nevertheless, like some other American leaders, including Anthony Wayne, Washington was not content to relegate spears to officers and advocated their use by some ordinary infantry soldiers as well. Those troops with bayonets obviously did not need to carry spears. However, Washington worried about the safety and effectiveness of his units of riflemen, since rifles had no bayonets. He reasoned that the spear would make a good auxiliary weapon for riflemen to help protect them against cavalry charges, so in early June 1777 he wrote to Daniel Morgan, leader of the famous Morgan's Riflemen:

> I have sent for spears, which I expect shortly to receive and deliver [to] you, as a defense against horse[men]; till you are furnished with these, take care not to be caught in such [a] situation as to give them any advantage over you.[22]

A week later, the spears arrived, but Washington was not totally satisfied with them. He had ideas for improvements, as he indicated in a letter to the American committee in charge of procuring weapons.

Benjamin Fowler, the man in charge of manufacturing the weapons, made a drawing that incorporated the commander in chief's suggestions and indicated that he would get right to work implementing them; furthermore, he would have the batch of five hundred spears intended for Morgan's Riflemen ready as soon as possible. Regrettably, no evidence survives to confirm that Morgan and his men actually used these spears in the Battle of Saratoga, which took place a few months later.

It is certain, however, that some American fighters used such spears in combat situations in the war. They played an especially prominent role in numerous naval engagements, in which spears were used liberally to supplement firearms and cutlasses. According to an account in a Pennsylvania newspaper, in a naval skirmish that took place in May 1776, "great execution was done by the spears. One man, with that weapon, is positive of having killed nine of the enemy."[23] In these ways, swords, axes, and spears, among the oldest weapons known to humanity, played their part in the emergence of the United States and other modern nations.

CHAPTER THREE

Battle Tactics Old and New

Perhaps the most common myth perpetuated about the American Revolution is that the war's tactics (battlefield maneuvers and methods) can best be characterized as a clash of old-fashioned, formal European tactics and unorthodox, informal American guerrilla tactics. According to this view, the Americans most often fought individually or in small groups and hid behind rocks and trees, well camouflaged by drab frontier garb. From these hiding places, they sniped at the British troops, who almost always walked along in the open in disciplined lines in bright red informs, unnecessarily exposing themselves to danger and death.

This myth is easily exposed for what it is by any straightforward examination of the actual events of the battles fought during the conflict. In most of these clashes, especially the larger ones, the opposing armies faced each other in the open in the traditional European manner. It is true that American troops did sometimes use guerrilla tactics, as in the cases of riflemen

sniping at British officers or patriots ambushing unsuspecting British units or raiding the houses of known loyalists. For the most part, these actions were carried out by members of the militia, ordinary citizens who fought on a temporary basis and then returned to their homes and farms. More often, however, groups of militia supplemented the ranks of the regular, standing American army. The American regulars trained in and adhered to the standard infantry and cavalry tactics of the day (although both the Americans and British employed cavalry rather sparingly in the war, partly because of the general ruggedness of the terrain). The upshot is that American soldiers, including militiamen, employed formal battle tactics more often than informal ones.

Harassment and Containment Tactics

Though formal battlefield maneuvers were the rule, the use of more informal guerrilla tactics by American militia units should by no means be discounted. In fact, such tactics were from time to time quite effective and advanced the American cause. This informal mode of fighting was largely a new phenomenon in modern warfare, so the British were unprepared for it. In the words of historian Jeremy Black, it reflected the unique situation of the rebellious colonies:

> The American war was the first example of a transoceanic conflict fought between a European colonial power and subjects of European descent, and the first example of a major revolutionary war, a struggle for independence in which the notion of the citizenry under arms played a crucial role. The creation of the new state was accompanied by the creation of a new type of army; both reflected a more dynamic and egalitarian [equal] society than that of Europe.[24]

Usually, American militia groups acting on their own used what is best described as harassment and containment tactics. On the one hand, they patrolled the countryside, guarding farms, villages, and supply depots from British foragers (supply gatherers). This severely restricted the ability of the British to live off the land and forced them to import more food from across the ocean, a more difficult and expensive proposition. Such tactics also contained the British army largely in the coastal sections of the country. Practically every time British troops marched inland from the sea, hundreds and sometimes thousands of militiamen and other locals rose up to fight them. Disconcerted, the British typically halted their inland advance.

The main reason this tactic worked so well against the British was that having to face a whole countryside of angry, armed

American militiamen repulse a British charge. The British were not used to dealing with local militias that could appear at a moment's notice.

BRUTAL ATTACKS ON LOYALISTS

One common tactic of American militiamen (and sometimes regular soldiers) was to threaten, restrain, or terrorize local loyalists, keeping them from supplying or otherwise helping the British. At times, particularly in the Carolinas during the last two years of the war, such antiloyalist tactics could be brutal and cruel, though the patriots maintained that they were necessary. In Autobiography of a Revolutionary Soldier, *James Collins, an American soldier who took part in several raids against loyalists, describes such a raid.*

We would meet at a time and place appointed, probably at a church, schoolhouse, or some vacant building, generally in the afternoon, lay off our circuit and divide into two or more companies and set off after dark. Wherever we found any Tories, we would surround the house. One party would force the doors and enter, sword in hand, extinguish all the lights if there were any, and suffer no lights to be made, when we would commence hacking the man or men that were found in the house, threatening them with instant death, and occasionally mak-ing a furious stroke as if to dispatch them at once. . . . Another party would mount the roof of the house and commence pulling it down. Thus, the dwelling house, smoke houses and kitchen, if any, were dismantled and torn down. . . . The poor fellows, perhaps expecting instant death, would beg hard for life, and make any promise on condition of being spared, while their wives or friends would join in their entreaties. . . . There were none of the poor fellows much hurt, only they were hacked about their heads and arms enough to bleed freely.

A group of American militiamen ambush enemy troops moving along a road.

people was completely new to them. In Europe, an army on the march could expect to move safely through the countryside until it met enemy troops and engaged in a pitched battle. The frightened local townspeople and peasants almost always laid low or ran away. Seeing the American countryside in arms made the British nervous, even fearful, so for most of the war they avoided venturing too far inland, preferring to stay near the coast. There, the closeness of their ships and supply lines made them feel safer.

Such fears were well founded. Sometimes the efforts of local militiamen and other patriots helped bring about a major British defeat and to end an important strategic campaign. A clear example occurred in 1777. Britain's General John Burgoyne led an army southward from Canada by way of Lake Champlain (on the border between New York and Vermont). His goal was to invade and conquer northern New York and the New England states. But Burgoyne soon encountered the awesome power of a countryside at arms. Seemingly out of nowhere, groups of local patriots harassed and attacked his supply trains. Large groups of militiamen also continually reinforced the ranks of American regulars, who otherwise would have been outnumbered and unable to stop the British advance. Writing to another British leader, Burgoyne complained:

Wherever the King's forces point, [American] militia, to the number of three or four thousand, assemble in twenty-four hours. They bring with them their subsistence [food and other supplies], etc., and, the alarm over, they return to their farms. . . . In all parts [of the countryside] the [rebels'] industry and management in driving cattle and removing corn [to keep these supplies out of British hands] are indefatigable [untiring] and certain. . . . [General Horatio] Gates [the American commander opposing Burgoyne] is now strongly posted . . . with an army superior to mine . . . [with] as many militia as he pleases.[25]

British troops on the march are attacked by American snipers. Sneak attacks by local militiamen were particularly effective against enemy supply trains and foragers.

Burgoyne was quite correct to worry that the harassment and containment tactics of the armed locals posed a clear and present danger. In fact, he lost so many men (through death, wounding, or desertion) that he finally could not go on; on October 17, 1777, he had no choice but to surrender to Gates.

Come Out and "Fight Like Men"

During the majority of the battles fought during Burgoyne's campaign through upstate New York, American militiamen fought alongside Gates's regulars. But isolated British units sometimes found themselves ambushed or sniped at by rebel militiamen acting on their own, especially in wooded areas. When that happened at various times and places in the war, the British were quick to label their opponents cowards who would not come out and "fight like men." One British soldier bitterly complained in 1775: "They are a cowardly set that will not fight [except] when fenced by trees, houses or trenches."[26]

Although such informal tactics seemed cowardly to most British regulars, American militiamen, who lacked the high degree of organization and training of British troops, saw them as the safer and more practical approach. This was particularly true of riflemen. These marksmen with their slow-loading guns were most effective when they fired from behind some kind of cover. At the Battle of Long Island, on August 27, 1776, a British captain, William Congreve, witnessed such tactics and later wrote:

I found the enemy numerous and supported by the 6-pounders [can-

non]. However, by plying them smartly with grapeshot their guns were soon drawn off, but the riflemen being covered by trees and large stones had very much the advantage of us, who were upon the open ground . . . [and had] not the [British] light infantry . . . come up [to help us] in time I believe we should all have been cut off.[27]

Similar informal tactics that took advantage of natural obstacles were employed by the American riflemen who defeated the British at King's Mountain in October 1780. "The orders were at the firing of the first gun," a sixteen-year-old rifleman, Thomas Young, later recalled,

for every man to raise a whoop, rush forward, and fight his way [up the hill] as best he could. When our division came up to the northern base of the mountain, Colonel Roebuck drew us a little to the left and commenced the attack. . . . Ben Hollingworth and myself took right up the side of the mountain, and fought from tree to tree, our way to the summit. I recollect I stood behind one tree and fired until the bark was nearly all knocked off, and my eyes pretty well filled with it.[28]

The Use of Linear Battle Tactics

As effective as they could be in certain situations, such informal guerrilla tactics were the exception rather than the rule during the war. For the most part, the opposing armies

At the Battle of King's Mountain, the Americans take advantage of natural cover while moving up toward fortified enemy positions.

met in the open and employed formal lines of musket-bayonet men, the infantry formation that dominated European warfare by the early 1700s. Such fighting came to be called linear warfare, since the term *linear* refers to the use of lines. By the time of the American Revolution, linear tactics had become a standard convention of war. Honorable generals and officers were expected to follow established rules, which were set down in minute detail in numerous military manuals and handbooks of the period. Indeed, the desire to uphold such honor was a major factor in the decision of the American commander in chief, George Washington, to employ linear tactics against the British.

In the early 1700s, it was customary for an army's infantrymen to form a line five ranks deep on the battlefield. But by the outset of the Revolution, the British had reduced the depth of their standard line to three or four ranks, and the Americans typically used only two ranks. Field artillery (cannons on movable carriages) was usually interspersed at intervals among the infantry. Cavalry units, their men armed with sabers and pistols, placed themselves behind or on the flanks (sides) of the infantry. "The basic objective," George Neumann explains,

was to pierce the opponent's ranks and disrupt the formation by frontal assault, or, better yet, to maneuver into a position of hitting on the flank to 'roll up' his battle line. . . . The battle usually

Linear Battle Tactics

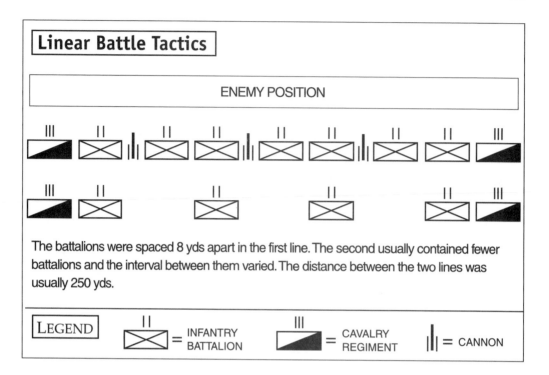

ENEMY POSITION

The battalions were spaced 8 yds apart in the first line. The second usually contained fewer battalions and the interval between them varied. The distance between the two lines was usually 250 yds.

LEGEND | = INFANTRY BATTALION | = CAVALRY REGIMENT | = CANNON

opened with artillery fire. Then one side would begin a steady disciplined advance with fixed bayonets, halt about 50 to 100 yards from their opponent and deliver one or a series of volleys—to which the others would reply. But since the inaccurate smoothbore musket was still more a defensive than an offensive weapon, the climax came when one side charged with the bayonet, backed when possible by sword-swinging cavalry. Despite advances in firearms, the classic 18th century battle was still decided by the clash of edged weapons at close quarters.[29]

The "long red line" of British musket-bayonet men in their red coats became a familiar sight to American fighters. British linear formations seemed especially formi-

dable to the rebels in the first two years of the war, when most American troops still lacked proper training in formal tactics. At times, the oncoming British appeared relentless and unstoppable; no matter how many times the patriots repulsed them, their ranks would re-form and renew the assault. This was the case in the famous Battle of Bunker Hill (actually fought on Breed's Hill) in Boston on June 17, 1775. The Americans, who had fortified the hilltop, watched grimly as the rows of redcoats marched toward them, keeping step to the beat of drummers. According to the account of an American defender, Peter Thacher:

Having sent out large flank guards in order to surround [the American position], they [the British] began a very slow march towards our lines. . . . The provincials [Americans] in the redoubt [fortified area on the hilltop] and the lines reserved their fire till the enemy had come within about ten or twelve yards and then discharged them at once upon them. The fire threw their body into very great confusion. . . . At length . . . the troops were again rallied and marched up to the entrenchments. The Americans reserved their fire and a second time put the regulars to flight, who once more retreated. . . . [The British regrouped and attacked still again and] the enemy advanced on three sides. . . . Can it be wondered at, then, that the word was given [for the Americans] to retreat? . . . With very great signs of exultation [triumph] the British troops . . . took possession of the hill.[30]

Untrained American troops fared even worse against British bayonet charges. At Camden, South Carolina, on August 16, 1780, the American militiamen who were supporting the regular army under Horatio Gates fled the field in disarray before the onrushing British bayonets. "I was among the nearest to the enemy," remembered Garret Watts, one of those who ran.

> We had orders to wait for the word to commence firing; the militia were in front and in feeble condition at that time. . . . I can state on oath that I believe my gun was the first gun fired, notwithstanding the orders, for we were close to the enemy, who appeared to maneuver [with their bayonets] in contempt of us, and I fired

American troops flee a British charge at Camden, South Carolina. The defeat was caused by lack of training and discipline among the Americans.

without thinking except that I might prevent the man opposite from killing me. The discharge and loud roar soon became general from one end of the lines to the other. Amongst other things, I confess I was amongst the first that fled. . . . Everyone I saw was about to do the same. It was instantaneous. There was no effort to rally, no encouragement to fight. Officers and men joined in the flight.[31]

American Mastery of Tactics

Fortunately, the American rout at Camden turned out to be the exception rather than the rule. It was largely attributable to the militia's lack of training and group discipline. In bold contrast, the American regulars at Camden stood their ground and maintained good order, though they were soundly defeated in the end. In fact, once the American regulars began training and drilling in linear tactics, they were usually able to stand up to their British counterparts. At the Battle of Long Island, fought on August 27, 1776, the Americans surprised the British by forming classic linear battle lines, as recalled by an unknown American participant in the fray:

The enemy then advanced to us, when Lord Stirling, who commanded, im-

---

MAJOR HOWE'S NEW TACTICS

In the early 1770s, Major General William Howe introduced some variations in discipline and tactics into standard British practices, believing that these would help British troops better adapt to fighting in North America. He trained his men to march and fight in two ranks, as well as the usual three or four, and to march into battle in open order (with at least an arm's length between individual soldiers). One of Howe's subordinates described the new rules (quoted in Stuart Reid's British Redcoat*).*

It is the Major General's wish, that the troops under his command may practice forming from two to three and four deep; and that they should be accustomed to charge in all those orders. In the latter orders, of the three and four deep, the files will, in course, be closer, so as to render a charge of the greatest force. The Major General also recommends to regiments the practice of dividing the battalions, by wings or otherwise, so that one line may support the other when an attack is supposed; and, when a retreat is supposed, that the first line may retreat through the intervals of the second, the second doubling up its divisions for the purpose, and forming again in order to check the enemy who may be supposed to have pressed the first line. The Major General would approve also of one division of a battalion attacking in the common open order of two deep, to be supported by the other compact division as a second line, in a charging order of three or four deep. The gaining the flanks also of a supposed enemy, by the quick movements of a division in common open order, while the compact division advances to a charge; and such other evolutions, as may lead the regiments to a custom of depending on and mutually supporting each other; so that should one part be pressed or broken, it may be accustomed to form again without confusion, under the protection of a second line, or any regular formed division.

At Cowpens, in South Carolina, Daniel Morgan leads a charge on British troops. Excellent training and discipline won the day for Americans.

mediately drew up in a line and offered them battle in the true English taste. The British then advanced within about 300 yards of us and began a very heavy fire from their cannon and mortars, for both the balls and shells flew very fast, now and then taking off a head. Our men stood it amazingly well, not even one showed a disposition to shrink. Our orders were not to fire till the enemy came within 50 yards of us; but when they perceived we stood their fire so coolly and resolutely, they declined coming any nearer, though treble [three times] our number.[32]

Although their battle lines and raw courage were impressive, the Americans eventually had to retreat from Long Island, which they did in well-ordered fashion. Yet their mastery of linear tactics, which had allowed them to face the legendary British lines without flinching, foreshadowed American victories to come. Perhaps no victory was more decisive and inspiring than that at Cowpens, in the Carolinas, on January 17, 1781. The sides were evenly matched and the battlefield open, flat, and unobstructed; military experts then and now agree that the American win was due almost entirely to a superior display of tactics and discipline, qualities that before this had usually been associated with the British army.

The British commander, cavalry leader Colonel Banastre Tarleton (who was notorious for his brutal terror raids on civilians), had a force of some eleven hundred British regulars and Tories. He arranged his battle line in the standard manner—with his infantry in the middle and cavalry units (in this case consisting of about fifty men each) on the flanks. In contrast, his opponent, the famous rifleman Daniel Morgan, had about one thousand men, including a mix of militia, regulars, and a few horsemen. Morgan organized his own troops into three lines. In the front he placed his militia; behind them were his regulars, commanded by Colonel John E. Howard; and in the rear were the cavalry, led by Colonel William Washington.

Seeing that Morgan had put his militia up front, the overconfident Tarleton was certain that the British would win the day. A hearty bayonet charge, he reasoned, would send the Americans packing, as had occurred at Camden. However, Morgan had wisely anticipated this possibility. He had told his militiamen, many of whom

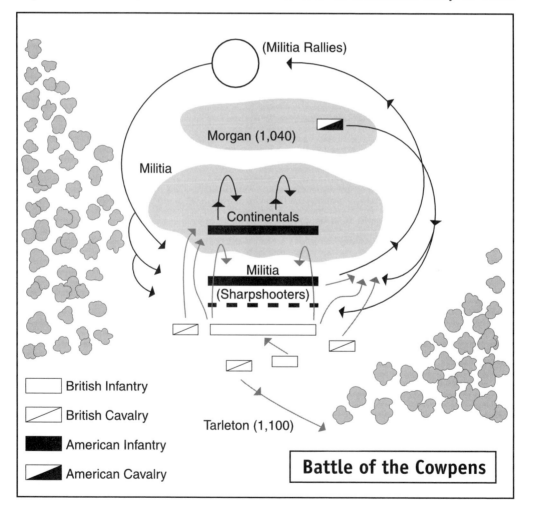

(Militia Rallies)

Morgan (1,040)

Militia

Continentals

Militia

(Sharpshooters)

British Infantry

British Cavalry

American Infantry

American Cavalry

Tarleton (1,100)

Battle of the Cowpens

were crack shots, to fire two volleys at the oncoming British and then swiftly move to the rear of the American army. The British would then have to contend with the better-trained and battle-hardened American regulars and horsemen. Morgan told his militiamen:

> Hold your fire till they're a hundred paces away. Give 'em two shots! Just two shots! Don't fire over their heads. . . . Move off and get around behind the hill. . . . Two shots right in the gizzard. Hit 'em in the head if it's easier! Same as shooting turkeys![33]

When the British front line came within a hundred yards of the American front line, Morgan's plan went into effect. The militiamen fired their two volleys, killing and wounding many in the front British rank, and then quickly moved toward the rear. At the same time, men from Tarleton's second rank filled the gaps in his front rank, which then marched forward at the American regulars. But to the surprise of the British, Morgan's troops suddenly pulled back, as if retreating. Sensing victory, the British regulars charged forward wildly, their ranks losing much of their order in the process. This was Morgan's and Howard's golden opportunity. They ordered their men to halt, turn, and fire on the onrushing enemy at nearly point-blank range. After this devastating barrage, the American regulars immediately launched into a spirited bayonet charge that shattered the British lines. At the same time, Morgan's

militiamen, now fully rested, stepped forward in orderly fashion from their rear position and fired at will into the crumbling British ranks. Desperate, Tarleton tried to use his small cavalry force to attack the American flanks, but Colonel Washington's own horsemen charged forward and routed them. In the words of one American soldier:

> In a few moments Colonel Washington's cavalry was among them like a whirlwind, and the poor fellows began to keel from their horses without being able to remount. The shock was so sudden and violent they could not stand it, and immediately betook themselves to flight.[34]

The outcome of the battle was for the Americans decisive and for the British shocking and demoralizing. Of Tarleton's force of 1,100 men, 100 had been killed, 200 wounded, and more than 600 captured. By contrast, American casualties were a mere 12 killed and 60 wounded. Tarleton was one of the few British who managed to escape (after he had engaged in a brief saber fight with Colonel Washington). In Tarleton's mind, his overwhelming defeat was merely a fluke; in the end, he and his countrymen would surely bring the rebels to their knees. But he was dead wrong. In only a few short years, the Americans had managed to master the tactics that had helped make the British army hugely effective and widely feared. This achievement would prove crucial to the ultimate American victory.

CHAPTER FOUR

The Urgent Need for Cannons

One of the biggest single logistical efforts made by the patriots in the American war for independence was to procure a sufficient number of cannons, then and now more formally called artillery or ordnance. Heroic though this effort was, the Americans were never able to match British artillery firepower. However, American cannons did do severe damage to the opposing army in key engagements, including the battle at Yorktown that forced the British to give up the conflict. So there is no denying that ordnance played an important role in the war.

American cannons were no different from British versions. (In fact, a large proportion of the artillery used by the patriots had been captured from the enemy.) Several major classes of artillery existed at the time. And each class featured a number of different sized cannons, as one size was often more practical or effective in a certain combat situation than others. One class of cannons, for instance, commonly called "field pieces," was most effective

on an open battlefield. Cannons in another class worked better for destroying walls and buildings during sieges. And still another class, referred to as naval ordnance, was designed or adapted to the peculiar needs of warships.

Regardless of how they were used, however, all types of artillery in use in the eighteenth century shared certain basic characteristics. First and foremost, the composition of their barrels was either iron or bronze. Also, these weapons were both smoothbore and muzzle-loading, like a musket. Another way that cannons resembled muskets was that both employed gunpowder to create an explosion that hurled a projectile at the enemy. And like a musketman, an artillery gunner loaded into his cannon a paper or cloth container called a cartridge, which held a premeasured amount of gunpowder.

The projectiles fired by the cannons of the American Revolution were made of metal and usually round. The single, solid, nonexplosive variety was informally called

BRITISH ARTILLERY GUNS

This chart, based on information compiled by scholar Ian Hogg (in his Armies of the American Revolution*), lists the various iron artillery guns used by the British during the American war for independence.*

Name	Caliber inches	Length feet	Length inches	Weight pounds	Range yards
3-pounder	2.90	4	6	725	1,400
6-pounder	3.67	6	0	1,650	1,500
6-pounder	3.67	8	0	2,200	1,500
9-pounder	4.20	7	0	2,300	1,800
9-pounder	4.20	7	6	2,425	1,800
12-pounder	4.62	7	6	2,925	1,800
12-pounder	4.62	8	6	3,125	1,800
12-pounder	4.62	9	0	3,200	1,800
12-pounder	4.62	9	6	3,400	1,800
18-pounder	5.29	9	0	4,000	2,300
18-pounder	5.29	9	6	4,200	2,300
24-pounder	5.82	9	0	4,750	2,400
24-pounder	5.82	9	6	4,900	2,400
24-pounder	5.82	10	0	5,200	2,400
32-pounder	6.41	9	6	5,500	2,900
32-pounder	6.41	10	0	5,800	2,900
42-pounder	6.95	9	6	6,500	3,100
42-pounder	6.95	10	0	6,700	3,100

a cannonball, but in military terms it was referred to as shot. A cluster of small iron balls that scattered after firing was called grapeshot, and a hollow ball filled with gunpowder designed to detonate on impact was called a shell.

All kinds of artillery had two other things in common. First, an artillery crew fired a cannon by inserting a lighted match into a vent in the rear. Second, firing such a weapon created a strong recoil that made it jump backward. So, the members of the crew had to push the cannon back into position before they could fire it again.

Guns, Howitzers, and Mortars

In the eighteenth century, crews manned one of three major kinds of artillery. The first was referred to simply as artillery "guns." A typical artillery gun had a long barrel in proportion to its caliber, was used for firing at

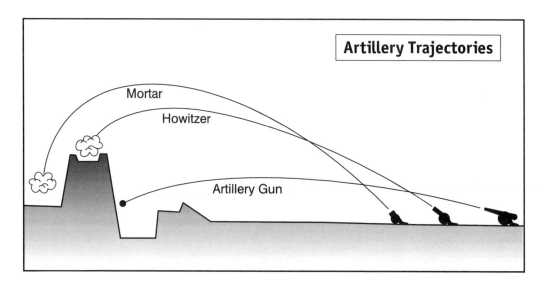

Artillery Trajectories

Mortar

Howitzer

Artillery Gun

targets within plain sight (as on the battle-field), and had a trajectory—the path taken by its projectile—that was flat and relatively low. A member of the gun crew aimed the weapon by sighting along two notches, one located near the muzzle, the other near the back. If he wanted less elevation (to make the cannon shoot even lower and flatter), he shoved one or more quoins, wooden wedges, under the back of the barrel, which lowered the angle of the muzzle. (A few of the guns used in the Revolution were equipped with a screw mechanism that eliminated the need for quoins.)

Artillery guns had more or less flat trajectories mainly because of the manner in which they rested in their carriages. A typical artillery gun carriage of the day consisted of an axle with two wheels attached to the ends. Resting on the middle of the axle were one or two pieces of timber, the backs of which were attached to a team of horses for transport or rested on the ground when the weapon was in use. The gun itself was fastened to

the tops of the timbers. So when the timbers holding the gun touched the ground in the back, the weapon could not be angled upward any higher.

The second major kind of ordnance, the howitzer, was capable of firing at a higher angle than a gun. This was partly because the howitzer had a larger caliber and shorter barrel, which made it easier to maneuver on a carriage. The bigger caliber and shorter barrel derived from the fact that the weapon was designed to fire shells. Being hollow, a shell was more fragile than solid shot, so the charge that propelled the shell had to be smaller to keep it from rupturing the shell's casing. The smaller the explosion, the shorter the barrel needed to accommodate it. Thus, the barrel length of an average howitzer was five to seven times its caliber, compared to fifteen to twenty-five times for a gun. Howitzers were the cannons of choice when one needed to fire over obstacles such as trees, houses, and low hills to reach the target.

The mortar, the third major kind of artillery, also fired a powder-filled shell rather than solid shot. A mortar was a short, stumpy cannon that fired at high angles, allowing its shells to pass over the high walls of forts and fortified towns and drop down on the desired target. Most mortars had barrels only one to three calibers long; thus, if a mortar's caliber was ten inches, its barrel was somewhere between ten and thirty inches long. This made the mortar by far the shortest of all cannons.

In contrast to the operational needs of guns and howitzers, the size of the powder charges used by mortar gunners varied considerably, depending on the range desired. "The whole concept of range determination changed when mortars were used," Ian Hogg explains.

Instead of having a fixed charge and varying the elevation of the piece to pitch the projectile to the desired range, the mortar used a fixed elevation—45 degrees—and varied the charge in order to alter the range.[35]

Because the mortar's angle of elevation was fixed, it was most practical to mount the weapon on a simple, stationary holder. Essentially, such a holder was a large block of wood with a curved recess carved in the top to accommodate the back end of the cannon. The whole assembly, weighing anywhere from about five hundred to eighty-five hundred pounds depending on the weapon's size,

These siege mortars rest near their original positions at Fort Ticonderoga. Such cannons utilized simple, stationary holders.

In this modern reenactment, men portraying artillerymen of the 1st Maryland Regiment prepare to fire their cannon.

could be lifted onto a wagon or boat for transport. Another consequence of the mortar's fixed elevation was the manner in which the gunner aimed it. According to Hogg:

> Sighting was done by scribing [carving] or painting a line down the top surface of the mortar barrel to coincide with [the] axis of the bore; this was aligned with the target by the gunner standing behind and holding a plumb-line in his hand. He sighted so that he saw the target on the far side of the plumb-line and had the axis line of the mortar barrel also in alignment with his plumb-line.[36]

Cannons on Wheels

There is no doubt that all three major types of cannon available in the late 1700s could be highly effective if aimed well and fired at the right angle. However, they all shared one major problem: Most of their barrels were extremely heavy and therefore difficult to transport overland. Few roads existed in the American colonies, and most were unpaved. Moreover, dirt roads and fields were often uneven, with holes and gullies, and when it rained, they turned to mud. As a result, the artillery carriages, dragged by horses, moved very slowly across the countryside, sometimes so slowly they could not keep up with the infantry. This meant that the foot soldiers had either to slow down to keep pace with their ordnance or move ahead of it and wait for it to catch up. Both options prolonged a campaign and frustrated the participants.

The general lack of mobility of artillery was addressed in contemporary military manuals dealing with these weapons. Perhaps the most famous and influential example was *A Treatise on Artillery*, first published in 1756 by John Muller, a German-born artillery master who had immigrated to England in his youth. Muller appreciated that most cannons were too heavy for the majority of existing roads and that the great number of horses involved further complicated matters. "All the carriages made use of in the artillery have shafts," he informed his readers. "And to prevent the great length of those that require a great number of horses, the rule is to draw [the artillery] by pairs [of horses standing] abreast."[37]

It was not only the cannons themselves that slowed an army down. The carriages bearing the weapons made up only part of a long artillery train that also included dozens or even hundreds of wagons carrying shot, shells, gunpowder, tools, spare parts, and

This drawing, dating from the eighteenth century, shows a powder cart from the side and from above. These carts accompanied cannons.

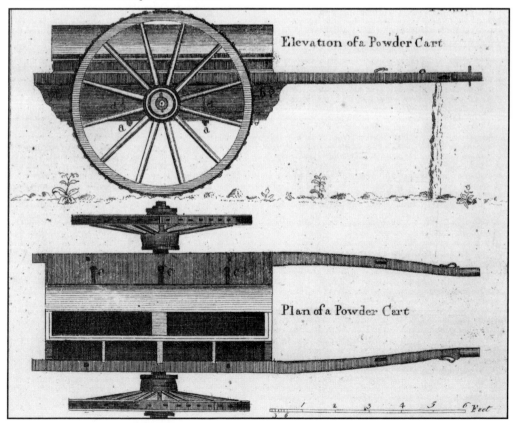

57

various other ordnance supplies. Military historian H.C.B. Rogers describes some of the typical vehicles that made up such a train:

A tumbril was a two-wheel cart to carry pioneers' and miners' tools. A powder cart also had two wheels, and contained shot lockers and space for four barrels of powder. An ammunition wagon was considerably larger, with four wheels. . . . The block carriage consisted of two long beams lengthwise on four wheels and was used to carry guns which were too heavy to be moved on their own carriages. A sling wagon was a four-wheel vehicle, with [a] rack and handle mounted in the center, for moving mortars and heavy guns over short distances from one position to another. The forge cart originally had two wheels, but it was so difficult to keep it steady that they were replaced by four. It was equipped with bellows, tool space, [an] iron plate for the fire place, [a] wooden trough for water, an iron plate for cinders, and another iron plate to stop the flame from setting fire to the cart. There was also a gin, a sort of portable crane for lifting ordnance on and off their carriages or mortar beds.[38]

The Americans Scramble to Find Cannons

Although the difficulty of moving an artillery train through the countryside was a daunting problem, it was actually the least of the worries facing American military plan-

DUELING ARTILLERY PIECES

Although field artillery was most often used on the open battlefield, it could also be effective in less formal skirmishes involving fewer troops and having no overall battle plan. Joseph P. Martin, an American soldier who took part in the chaotic fighting on Long Island in 1776, left behind this account (in his book Private Yankee Doodle*) of dueling artillery pieces in such a skirmish.*

We overtook a small party of the artillery, here dragging a heavy twelve-pounder upon a field carriage, sinking half way to the naves [wheel hubs] in the sandy soil. They plead[ed] hard for some of us to assist them to get in their piece [i.e., move it closer to the action]; our officers, however, paid no attention to their entreaties, but pressed forward towards a creek, where a large party of Americans and British were engaged. By the time we arrived, the enemy had driven our men into the creek, or rather mill-pond (the tide being up), where such as could swim got across; those that could not swim, and could not procure anything to buoy them up, sunk. The British, having several field pieces stationed by a brick house, were pouring the canister [shells] and grape[shot] upon the Americans like a shower of hail. They would doubtless have done them much more damage than they did but for the twelve-pounder mentioned above; the men, having gotten it within sufficient distance to reach them, and opening a fire upon them, soon obliged them to shift their quarters.

ARTILLERYMEN RECEIVE THEIR OFFICIAL UNIFORMS

In this excerpt from volume one of General Washington's Army, *scholar Marko Zlatich describes the official uniforms ordered by Henry Knox for the soldiers manning the new artillery corps he commanded. Until October 1778, when the first large batch of uniforms was distributed, the outfits worn by most members of American artillery crews were not standardized.*

Officers received regimental coats and brown breeches [pants]. For non-commissioned officers and drummers, Knox requested two-inch wide white leather sword belts to wear over the shoulder. Hats for the whole brigade were to be cocked [have their brims turned up in two or three places] without being cut, and ornamented with a piece of bearskin. . . . Artillery clothing for the campaign of 1779 [included] suits of black faced with scarlet, with yellow trimmings and lined in white. Coats for corporals, gunners, and bombardiers [ammunition men] were to have knots. . . . In April and May 1778, [the] 1st Continental Artillery Regiment received . . . 221 blue coats with red lapels, 74 striped waistcoats and pairs of breeches and 30 red jackets and pairs of breeches. Two Maryland companies, that joined the 1st Regiment in July, were also uniformed in blue faced scarlet.

This drawing depicts uniforms worn by American artillerymen.

ners at the outset of the Revolution. Much more pressing was a general lack of good ordnance in the former colonies. Just as disconcerting was the reality that no formal artillery corps or organization existed in America, a shortcoming that did not bode well for the patriots' war effort.

As it turned out, a small number of patriots fortunately had some knowledge of artillery. One of these men, a Bostonian named Henry Knox, caught George Washington's attention. After the Battle of Bunker Hill, in which Knox took part, Washington asked him to create an American artillery force. Almost immediately, Knox showed that he was the right man for the job. He managed to transport some fifty cannons captured from the British at Fort Ticonderoga, in upstate New York, to Boston, where they were eventually instrumental in driving the British out of the city.

Knox then turned his attention to organizing the widely scattered colonial artillerymen and collecting enough ordnance for them to use. In mid-1776, Knox created four artillery regiments. Each regiment eventually consisted of ten companies, the size of a company depending on the number and caliber of the ordnance it possessed. A fairly typical artillery company had between six and ten artillery guns or howitzers. To find these weapons, at first Knox had to resort to the proverbial beg, borrow, and steal method. His men scoured the colonies collecting whatever they could find and whenever possible confiscated British cannons.

Knox fully realized that these makeshift methods would not do in the long run, and he pressed for American forges to manufacture their own cannons. Rising to the challenge, one Pennsylvania forge produced about sixty artillery pieces in 1776. However, Knox also recognized that cannon-making facilities in different areas would turn out ordnance of widely varying sizes and calibers, making it more difficult for him to standardize American artillery. So he established a central cannon factory in Springfield, Massachusetts, where the dimensions and calibers of ordnance were tightly supervised.

Henry Knox and his men drag several cannons overland from Fort Ticonderoga to Boston. These weapons played a key role in dislodging the British from Boston.

Most historians agree that Knox's artillery units soon became the most effective branch of the infant American military establishment. This was partly due to efficient organization and just plain hard work. But innovation was also a key factor. The Americans tried to increase the mobility of the ordnance used to support infantry on the battlefield by making smaller, lighter, more portable cannons. These came to be called galloper guns, some of which could be pulled by a single horse. (However, some of the weapon's mobility was offset by the fact that its ammunition had to be carried in wagons, which were as slow as ever.)

How Cannons Were Used

The use of artillery on the battlefield during the Revolution was usually not decisive, even considering such factors as Britain's superior number of cannons, Knox's enormous efforts to build an American artillery corps, and innovations such as galloper guns. In general, military commanders employed guns and howitzers in two ways. First, these weapons protected an army's deployment onto the battlefield. In other words, a general needed to move his infantry and cavalry units into the desired positions without risking harassment or sudden attack by the enemy, and a screen of artillery field pieces provided cover for these troop movements. Artillery pieces also took part in actual combat, most often by firing on enemy formations, softening them up for attacks by infantry and cavalry.

A major factor in the effectiveness of such tactics was, of course, the mobility of the artillery involved. Realizing this, artillery crews of the American Revolution sometimes attempted to implement the tactical advances recently introduced by

Prussian leader Frederick the Great in Europe's Seven Years' War (1756–1763). In fact, the American development of galloper guns was directly inspired by Frederick's innovations, summarized here by military historian Albert Manucy:

> To keep pace with cavalry movements, [Frederick] developed a horse artillery that moved rapidly along with the cavalry. His field artillery had only light guns and howitzers. With these improvements he could establish small batteries at important points in the battle line, open the fight, and protect the deployment of his columns with light guns. What was equally significant, he could change the position of his batteries according to the course of the action.[39]

In such combat situations, field artillery gunners sometimes fired randomly into the enemy ranks, hoping to wreak whatever havoc they could. But the better generals and artillery commanders tried to concentrate their fire on points of weakness in the enemy lines. They were influenced by a noted French artillery expert, the Chevalier du Teil, who had written, "It is necessary to multiply the artillery on the points of attack which ought to decide the victory." To secure "decisive results," he said, "it is necessary to assemble the greatest number of troops, and a great quantity of artillery, on the points where one wishes to force the enemy." Furthermore, to make sure these are the weak points, one should distract the enemy by implementing "false attacks" at other points in his line.[40]

Gunners of an American artillery emplacement in the Battle of Monmouth take orders from their unit commander (left-center with sword).

Standing Up to Fear of Artillery Barrages

Artillery field pieces were effective not merely because of the physical damage they did to the enemy. When applied properly, these weapons could also frighten, confuse, and demoralize the opposing troops. A Prussian soldier who encountered Austrian artillery in a battle fought just prior to the outbreak of the American Revolution left behind this riveting testimony:

A storm of shot and howitzer shells passed clear over our heads, but more than enough fell in the ranks to smash a large number of our men. . . . I glanced aside just once and I saw an NCO [noncommissioned officer] torn apart by a shell nearby.

The sight was frightful enough to take away my curiosity. . . . [Then we advanced] through long corn, which reached as far as our necks, and as we came nearer we were greeted with a hail of canister [shells] that stretched whole clumps of our troops on the ground.[41]

Such barrages of artillery shot were enough to unnerve even the most battle-hardened soldier. However, cases of individuals who openly defied and lived through such dangers have been documented. One of the most famous such episodes in the American Revolution occurred at the Battle of Monmouth, in New Jersey, in June 1778. Molly Pitcher, a camp follower who supplied the American troops with water, bravely took over her husband's job as artillery gunner when he was wounded and then herself had a narrow brush with death. The following eyewitness account is attributed to American soldier Joseph P. Martin in his memoir of the war:

[The] woman . . . attended with her husband at the piece the whole time. While in the act of reaching for a cartridge and having one of her feet as far before the other as she could step, a cannon shot from the enemy passed directly between her legs without doing any other damage than carrying away all the lower part of her petticoat. Looking at it with apparent unconcern, she observed that it was lucky it did not pass a little higher, for in that case it might have carried away something else, and [she] continued her occupation.[42]

Even more renowned was a similar incident involving the American commander in chief. During the furious, weeks-long American and French artillery barrage of the British at Yorktown in September and October 1781, American soldier John Suddarth witnessed a remarkable act of courage

When Molly Pitcher's husband was wounded during the Battle of Monmouth, she took his place in his cannon crew.

by George Washington. "During a tremendous cannonade [artillery barrage] from the British," Suddarth later recalled,

General Washington . . . took his [spy]glass and mounted the highest, most prominent, and most exposed point of our fortifications, and there stood exposed to the enemy's fire, where shot seemed flying almost as thick as hail and were instantly demolishing portions of the embankment around him for ten or fifteen minutes, until he had completely satisfied himself of the purposes of the enemy. During this time his aides, etc., were remonstrating [arguing] with him with all their earnestness against this exposure of his person and once or

George Washington touches off a round of cannon shot during the American siege of Yorktown in October 1781.

American cannons blast away at British positions in Yorktown in September 1781.

twice drew him down. He severely reprimanded them and resumed his position.[43]

A Cannon Assault Ends the War

By far the most destructive and frightening kinds of artillery barrages were those of besieged forts and towns by mortars, sometimes supplemented by howitzers. Perhaps the most memorable example in the war was the American attack on Yorktown, facing Chesapeake Bay in southern Virginia, an action that brought about the British surrender and ended the war. By March 1781, the Americans had won a succession of victories in the Carolinas. This forced the leading British general,

Charles Cornwallis, to move his forces to Virginia, and in April he established new headquarters at Yorktown. Soon, a large allied force of American and French troops commanded by General Washington converged on Yorktown. Cornwallis now found himself trapped between the American and French troops on his land side and a fleet of French ships, armed with cannons, anchored in the bay.

On September 28, 1781, allied American and French cannons opened fire on Yorktown from both sides. On the land side, the artillery pieces were at first placed at a distance of a thousand yards. But as the days passed and the enemy's defenses weakened, the Americans moved their cannons closer. By October 10 the barrage was more intense than ever. Cornwallis was so worried about being hit by the shot and shells that he moved into a makeshift bunker dug beneath the garden of the house he had been using. Yet the British gunners in the town must be credited for firing back, even if their shells did little damage. An American surgeon, James Thacher, later recalled:

> From the 10th to the 15th, a tremendous and incessant firing from the American and French batteries is kept up, and the enemy return the fire, but with little effect. A red-hot shell from the French battery set fire to the *Charon*, a British 44-gun ship, and two or three smaller vessels at anchor in the river, which were consumed in the night. . . . The ships were enwrapped in a torrent of fire, which spread with vivid brightness among the combustible rigging, and running with amazing rapidity to the tops of the several masts, while all around was thunder and lightning from our numerous cannon and mortars, and in the darkness of the night, presented one of the most sublime and magnificent spectacles which can be imagined.[44]

As the American and French artillery continued to pound the town with increasing fury, the modest efforts of the British defenders eventually proved fruitless. A German officer serving under Cornwallis later described the devastating allied barrage of October 17:

> At daybreak the enemy bombardment resumed, more terribly strong than ever before. They fired from all positions without letup. Our command, which was in the Hornwork, could hardly tolerate the enemy bombs, howitzer, and cannonballs any longer. There was nothing to be seen but bombs and cannonballs raining down on our entire line.[45]

This virtual rain of death convinced Cornwallis that his position was hopeless, and two days later he surrendered his entire army to General Washington. After this major defeat, brought about almost entirely by artillery fire, the British no longer had the stomach to go on. The war was over and Britain's claim to its former American colonies was at an end.

CHAPTER FIVE

David Versus Goliath on the High Seas

The naval confrontation between Britain and America during the American Revolution was, in the words of prestigious twentieth-century American historian Henry Commager, "a nautical version of David and Goliath."[46] That this characterization is largely true can be seen by the great disparity in naval strength that existed between the two powers. At the beginning of the conflict, and indeed throughout the duration of the fighting, the British were nothing less than the masters of the world's seas. In 1775 the Royal Navy had 131 warships carrying between 60 and 100 guns (naval cannons), 98 more with from 20 to 56 guns, and 41 smaller fighting vessels, for a total of 270. By the conclusion of the conflict, Britain's war fleet included 478 ships, 174 of which carried 60 to 100 guns and 198 of which had 20 to 56 guns. In addition, Britain's fleet of cargo vessels was more than 7,000 strong throughout the war.

The British did not commit all of these vessels to the war effort against the former American colonies. Britain's navy also guarded England's coasts and carried out missions around the world. Nevertheless, when the British lost warships or cargo vessels in American waters, they had the resources to replace such vessels promptly. Thus, at any given moment during the war, large numbers of British warships patrolled the east coast of North America, blockading American ports and preventing badly needed supplies and other overseas aid from reaching the former colonies. Britain's warships also carried troops swiftly from one strategic location to another.

The American naval situation was quite the opposite from that of Britain. When the conflict began, the patriots had no official navy and no long-standing naval institutions and traditions of their own. At first, the Americans were able to muster only a few dozen small schooners (sailboats) and cargo ships, most of which had no cannons. Luckily, Congress wasted no time in creating the so-called Continental Navy, which started a crash program for building warships. However, these vessels were far fewer in number and carried markedly fewer cannons than those in the British navy. Of the American war vessels, only four carried forty or more guns, and most had fewer than twenty-eight guns. Furthermore, launching even this extremely small fleet constituted an enormous undertaking for a new nation with a small population and a still tiny and loosely organized military establishment. As naval historian Jack Coggins points out:

During the Revolution both warships and smaller boats were often used as troop transports.

Individual ships of small size might be built and equipped, but the construction of a large fleet of ships capable of lying in the line of battle, with their attendant frigates [warships with 20 to 44 guns] and smaller craft, was entirely beyond any but a first-class power. For the revolted colonies, torn with war and internal dissentions and . . . all but penniless, to attempt such a thing was out of the question.[47]

Moreover, while most British naval officers had combat experience, very few of their American counterparts had seen action on the high seas. "The raw material was there," Coggins continues. A number of the American ship captains and their junior officers "were men of great experience and skill." Also, "there were many colonials capable of commanding a merchant vessel." The problem was that few of these individuals "had actually been in combat."[48]

Largely because Americans lacked sheer numbers of warships, guns, and experienced naval officers, by 1781 almost all of their larger vessels had been sunk or captured. It cannot be denied, however, that the captains and crews of these ships had fought bravely and made a real difference in the war effort. During the few short years they had been afloat, they had disrupted enemy communications and overseas commerce, raided the coasts of the British Isles and various British colonies, hindered enemy troop movements (thereby saving several American states from being overrun), and sunk or captured some two hundred British ships, mostly cargo vessels. Also, American

U.S. WARSHIPS OF THE AMERICAN REVOLUTION CARRYING 24 OR MORE CANNONS

Name of Ship	Number of Cannons	Source	Fate
Alfred	24	Bought	Captured
Raleigh	32	Built	Captured
Hancock	32	Built	Captured
Warren	32	Built	Destroyed
Washington	32	Built	Destroyed
Randolph	32	Built	Destroyed
Providence	28	Built	Captured
Trumbull	28	Built	Captured
Congress	28	Built	Destroyed
Virginia	28	Built	Captured
Effingham	28	Built	Destroyed
Boston	24	Built	Captured
Montgomery	24	Built	Destroyed
Delaware	24	Built	Captured
Indien	40	Built	Sold
Deane	32	Built	Name changed to Hague; retired in 1783
Queen of France	28	Bought	Destroyed
Alliance	32	Built	Sold
Confederacy	32	Built	Captured
Bonhomme Richard	42	Bought	Destroyed
Pallas	32	Borrowed	Returned after war
Serapis	44	Captured	Sold
America	74	Built	Given to France in 1786
Bourbon	36	Built	Sold

privateers sank or captured another six hundred enemy merchant ships.

The Need to Build a Navy

From a modern vantage point, it seems only natural that the patriots would construct a war fleet to do as much damage as possible to enemy ships. However, the reality is that the American navy almost never made it off the drawing boards. At first, many of the founding fathers were convinced that building a navy was a waste of time and money, since any attempt to oppose the mighty Royal Navy would surely be suicidal. Finally, in late August 1775, one colonial assembly—that of Rhode Island—had the gumption to make a formal proposal to Congress that warships be built.

About two months later, Congress appointed a committee of three—John Adams, John Langdon, and Silas Deane—to consider naval preparedness. "The opposition was very loud and vehement," Adams later remembered.

> Some of my colleagues appeared greatly alarmed by [the idea of sending warships against the British]. . . . It was [like] an infant taking a mad bull by the horns; and what was more profound and remote, it was said it would ruin the character and corrupt the morals of our seamen.[49]

Fortunately, the committee ignored these objections and did its job. On October 30, 1775, Congress added four more members to the group and officially dubbed it the Naval Committee. Adams and the others worked quickly. On December 11, 1775, they recommended to Congress that the patriots build thirteen warships—five with 32 guns, five with 28 guns, and three with 24 guns—all to be ready for action in 1776.

Washington's Army Fleet

Meanwhile, several members of the committee pointed out a more pressing need, namely for ships to intercept British supplies bound for Boston and other American cities. Luckily, George Washington had already foreseen this necessity. Between early September and late November 1775, he had acquired seven small merchant vessels and outfitted them with whatever ordnance he could find. (This army-controlled squadron was one of three small squadrons that supplemented the main oceangoing

A replica of the Chasseur, *an American schooner, is shown above.*

fleet; the other two patrolled Lake Champlain, in upstate New York, and the Mississippi River, respectively.)

The first ship in Washington's fleet was the *Hannah*, a schooner outfitted with four small cannons. Its captain, Nicholas Broughton, received the following instructions:

> You . . . are hereby directed to take the command of a detachment of said Army and proceed on board the schooner *Hannah* . . . on a cruise against such vessels as may be found on the high seas or elsewhere, bound inwards and outwards, to or from Boston . . . and to take and seize all [British] vessels laden with soldiers,

arms, ammunition or provisions . . . or which you shall have good reason to suspect are in such service.[50]

To modern eyes, these may seem like rather tall orders for a ship so small and lacking in ordnance. Yet they show both how seriously patriot leaders such as Washington and Adams took the British threat and the degree of professionalism they wanted to instill in the emerging American naval forces. In spite of their obvious material shortcomings, Broughton and other American ship captains were expected to meet high standards and impose and maintain efficient organization and strict discipline aboard their vessels. To ensure this, on November 28, 1775, the

Naval Committee issued an official set of naval rules and regulations. "The Commanders of all ships and vessels belonging to the Thirteen United Colonies," the document begins,

are strictly required to show in themselves a good example of honor and virtue to their officers and men, and to be very vigilant in inspecting the behavior of all such as are under them, and to . . . suppress all . . . immoral and disorderly practices; and also, such as are contrary to the rules of discipline and obedience, and to correct those who are guilty of the same according to the usage of the sea.[51]

STRICT RULES FOR THE NEW AMERICAN NAVY

A number of strict rules of discipline and obedience were spelled out by the Naval Committee in its Rules for the Regulation of the Navy of the United Colonies of North-America, *issued in 1775. The following are some of them.*

If any shall be heard to swear, curse or blaspheme the name of God, the Captain is strictly enjoined to punish them for every offence, by causing them to wear a wooden collar or some other shameful badge of distinction, for so long a time as he shall judge proper. If he [the offender] be a commissioned officer he shall forfeit one shilling for each offence, and a warrant or inferior officer, six-pence. He who is guilty of drunkenness (if a seaman) shall be put in irons until he is sober, but if an officer, he shall forfeit two days pay. No Commander shall inflict any

punishment upon a seaman beyond twelve lashes upon his bare back with a cat of nine-tails [a kind of whip]; if the fault shall deserve a greater punishment, he is to apply to the Commander in Chief of the navy in order to the trying of him by a court-martial, and in the mean time he may put him under confinement. . . . Any officer, seaman or marine, who shall begin to excite, cause, or join in any mutiny or sedition in the ship to which he belongs on any pretence whatsoever, shall suffer death or such other punishment as a court-martial shall direct. None shall presume to quarrel with, or strike his superior officer, on pain of such punishment as a court-martial shall order to be inflicted. . . . All murder shall be punished with death. All robbery and theft shall be punished at the discretion of a court-martial.

Cannons for the New Warships

The committee's new rules and regulations failed to address one key factor, one that was ultimately more crucial than any amount of professionalism and discipline on the part of the ships' captains and crewmen. Above all else, American ships needed effective ordnance, since in naval cannonry the British outnumbered them more than a hundred to one. At the outset of the war, the rebels possessed few large cannons of any kind, and Washington needed most of these for his land army. To equip his small fleet of schooners, Washington managed to borrow or capture a few small artillery pieces.

On the other hand, outfitting the new frigates Congress had ordered to the main fleet was far more problematic. Colonial foundries were simply not up to the task of producing large, standardized, reliable naval ordnance in large quantities. To make up for this shortfall, the rebels captured whatever British cannons they could and bought more from France (although many of the French guns turned out to be outdated and sometimes unreliable). Meanwhile, Benedict Arnold, who was in charge of the small Lake Champlain fleet, armed several of his vessels with artillery pieces captured from the British at Fort Ticonderoga.

Even when American ships managed to find enough cannons, there was no guarantee they would be effective in battle. Seamen trained in firing cannons were in short supply in the colonies. Also, such guns were cumbersome and very difficult to aim, especially from the rolling deck of a ship. Sights were either nonexistent or inefficient; the large amount of windage in the barrels of naval ordnance practically ensured that the paths of the cannonballs would be off target; and in the time lag between the order to "fire!" and the actual explosion of the charge, both the attacking ship and its opponent moved in unpredictable ways, further hindering accuracy. Because of these factors, the warships of the day were equipped with as many big guns as possible. The hope was that a massive artillery barrage would do enough damage to the enemy to make up for the lack of accuracy of individual cannons.

In addition to the problems relating to accuracy, naval gunners faced considerable difficulties simply in firing their weapons. The typical loading and firing sequence included many steps, all of which were important. If any one of them was done improperly, the gun might misfire, injuring the gunners, or not fire at all. According to Jack Coggins:

> On being called to quarters (action stations) by beat of drum or bugle call, the gun crew first cast off the lashings with which the guns were always securely fastened to the ship's side when not in use. . . . The gun was run in and the tampion, or wooden plug used to keep out spray and moisture, was taken out of the muzzle. A cartridge—a cylindrical bag of powder, often made of flannel—was brought up to the gun from the magazine below decks. . . . The cartridge was rammed all the way down the bore, and a ball was . . . rammed down on the charge. . . .

Pictured are naval cannons in the gundeck of the USS Constitution *(left) and beside the HMS* Victory *(below)*

A lighted slow match, made of cotton wick soaked in lye, or some other substance, was twisted about a forked stick some three feet long (the linstock). . . . When the gun captain thought his piece was well and truly laid on the target he side-stepped smartly to avoid the backward rush of the cannon in recoil and ordered the glowing end of the match brought down on the vent. There was a poof of flame and smoke from the vent, followed almost instantaneously by the flash and roar of the gun, which ran back until checked by the breeching [a heavy rope that secured the gun to the ship's side].[52]

Sheer Audacity Pays Off

Though British naval gunners faced these same problems, British ships had far more ordnance and larger numbers of trained seamen than American ships did. But while the rebels were clearly outgunned, they did not shy away from adopting bold strategies and tactics. Sometimes their sheer audacity paid off.

The first American naval mission of the war—that of Captain Broughton and his *Hannah*—is a case in point. The little warship left port on September 5, 1775, and on its second day out spotted a large British merchantman, the *Unity*, bound for Boston and heavily loaded with lumber and other valuable supplies. Broughton later reported how he accomplished the first

American capture of an enemy ship in the war:

> I saw a ship under my lee quarter [away from the wind]; I perceived her to be a large ship. I tacked and stood back for the land; soon after I put about and stood towards her again and found her a ship of no force [equipped with few or no cannons]. I came up with her, hailed, and asked where she came from; was answered, from Piscataqua, and bound to Boston. I told him he must bear away and go into Cape Ann [north of Boston]; but being very loath [because he was reluctant], I told him if he did not I should fire on her. On that she bore away and I have brought her safe into Cape Ann Harbor.[53]

In a similar manner, other small craft in Washington's squadron scored some modest successes in the months that followed.

"Never Had Any Force . . . Died More Gloriously"

In light of these surprising early successes, American naval planners decided to adopt even more daring strategies for some of the larger American warships after they were completed in 1776. Patriot leader Robert Morris urged John Paul

John Paul Jones's ship, Ranger *(left), moves in on the British warship,* Drake, *in April 1778. Jones captured the enemy vessel in British waters.*

Jones's Bonhomme Richard *slugs it out with the forty-four-gun British warship* Serapis. *The*

Jones, one of the more experienced captains in the American fleet, to attack the British in the West Indies and Florida in an effort to draw British warships away from American cities. Morris wrote:

> Destroying their settlements, spreading alarms, showing and keeping up a spirit of enterprise that will oblige them to defend their extensive possessions at all points, is of infinitely more consequence to the United States of America than all the plunder that can be taken. . . . It has long been clear to me that our infant fleet cannot protect our own coasts; and the only effectual relief it can afford us is to attack the enemy's defenseless places and thereby oblige them

to station more of their ships in their own countries, or to keep them employed in following ours, and either way, we are relieved so far as they do it.[54]

Employing this strategy, Jones scored some early successes and then boldly went even further by carrying the naval war to the enemy's very shores. He executed a series of audacious raids on English and Irish coasts beginning in April 1778 and captured a small British warship, the *Drake*, in the process. The following year, he captured seventeen enemy merchant vessels off the British coast and then took on the British warship *Serapis*, outfitted with forty-four guns. In a furious battle, Jones's smaller ship, the

Bonhomme Richard, exchanged fire with the enemy at point-blank range. Then, when the captain of the *Serapis* called for the Americans to surrender, Jones delivered his now famous reply: "I have not yet begun to fight!"[55] The battle continued and two hours later it was the *Serapis* that surrendered to Jones.

Meanwhile, no less bold was the American confrontation with the British on Lake Champlain. In October 1776, at Valcour Bay, Benedict Arnold's small naval squadron engaged a superior enemy force in hopes of delaying a British invasion of New York and New England from the north. As Arnold himself described the David-and-Goliath-like encounter:

Yesterday morning at eight o'clock, the enemy's fleet . . . appeared off Cumberland Head. We immediately prepared to receive them. . . . At eleven o'clock they ran under the lee of Valcour and began the attack. The schooner, by some bad management, fell to leeward and was first attacked; one of her masts was wounded, and her rigging shot away. The captain thought prudent to run her [aground] on the point of Valcour, where all the men were saved. . . . At half-past twelve the engagement became general and very warm [intense]. Some of the enemy's ships . . . continued a very

Depicted is the naval battle on Lake Champlain, in October 1776, which the Americans lost.

hot fire with round and grape-shot until five o'clock, when they thought proper to retire to about six or seven hundred yards distance, and continued the fire until dark. The [American vessels] *Congress* and *Washington* have suffered greatly; the latter lost her first lieutenant killed, captain and master wounded. The *New York* lost all her officers, except her captain. The *Philadelphia* was hulled [poked with holes] in so many places that she sunk in about one hour after the engagement was over.[56]

In the long run, it proved inconsequential that the Americans were swept from the lake and lost the battle. Of more strategic importance was that the extra time the British had taken to amass their lake fleet and square off with Arnold had forced them to put off and eventually cancel their invasion. In the words of noted nineteenth century naval historian Alfred T. Mahan, "Never had any force, big or small, lived to better purpose, or died more gloriously. . . . [Later crucial American victories were] due to the invaluable year of delay secured to them by their little navy on Lake Champlain."[57]

CHAPTER SIX

The Secret War: American and British Spies

The gathering of intelligence (useful information about the enemy) and other spy activities were among the most powerful weapons used by both sides, especially by the patriots, in the American Revolution. One reason that the Americans saw an urgent need for developing a spy network was the existence of large numbers of loyalists in their midst. The concern was that any loyalist might at any time act as a spy by collecting vital information about the patriots and passing it on to the British.

This threat of spying by loyalists was very real and potentially hugely damaging, since the number of loyalists was larger than most people today realize. Of about 2.5 million people living in the new nation in 1776, leading patriot John Adams estimated that about a third, or nearly 850,000, were loyal to the king. (Another third, he said, were patriots like himself. The rest did not care who governed them.) And more than 50,000 loyalists fought in the British ranks against the patriots. Therefore, the American Revolution was not only a war for independence but also a true civil war in which neighbors fought neighbors. In addition, neighbors spied on each other. It is not surprising, then that only a few months after the opening battles of the conflict (at Lexington and Concord), Congress recognized the need for countering the threat of enemy spies as well as collecting valuable intelligence about enemy forces.

An Urgent Need for Good Intelligence

To that end, on November 29, 1775, Congress created the Committee of Secret Correspondence. Its members included some of the major American founding fathers: Pennsylvania's Benjamin Franklin, Virginia's Benjamin Harrison, and New York's Robert Livingston. Two years later, Congress changed the committee's name to the Committee of Foreign Affairs, though its secret activities remained the same. Among these were sending secret agents behind enemy

A VERITABLE ARMY OF SPIES

In a very real way, the British benefited from having a veritable army of spies in the form of American loyalists. Loyalists lived everywhere—in all the cities and throughout the countryside—and they often watched their neighbors and reported what they saw to the British. As noted historians Henry S. Commager and Richard B. Morris point out (in this excerpt from volume one of The Spirit of 'Seventy-Six), *many patriots felt threatened enough to resort to harsh measures against loyalists.*

The very strength of loyalism in America condemned it to persecution. Had the loyalists been few in number, weak and disorganized, the patriots might have ignored them, or have contented themselves with making sure that they could do no harm. But they were numerous and powerful, strong enough at times to take the offensive against the patriots and endanger the success of the Revolution. It was not, therefore, surprising that even before Independence the patriots moved to frustrate, intimidate, punish and, if possible, wipe out loyalism. . . . The treatment of the loyalists was harsh, but harshness has almost always characterized the treatment of those who were on the wrong, or losing, side of a revolution. From the point of view of the patriots, the loyalists were traitors and therefore worse than open enemies. Nor can the judicious historian deny that the patriots had considerable justification for their attitude and their actions. Loyalists were numerous enough to be dangerous; they did in fact give aid to the enemy; many were spies and informers, many more sold food supplies to the British; thousands fought in the British ranks.

lines and abroad to collect intelligence and analyzing that information and making estimates of enemy troop strengths. The committee's agents also conducted covert (undercover) operations, including sabotage; spread misinformation to deceive the enemy; created and broke codes designed to hide secret information; and intercepted and opened private mail. Finally, the committee secretly funded privateers (armed, privately owned ships) to capture or destroy enemy ammunition and supplies.

In addition to this initial committee, Congress appointed another committee in June 1776 to decide what to do about British agents caught spying on the Americans. Its members included John Adams, Thomas Jefferson, and Robert Livingston, among others. At the time, no law existed to handle cases of civilian espionage (spying), and American military leaders felt that the existing punishments for military spying were not severe enough. In August, the committee made its recommendations to Congress, which immediately enacted the first U.S. espionage act. It prescribed the death penalty for foreigners caught spying in the United States.

Before long, however, it became clear that the new law did not go far enough. Several leading patriots felt that those subject to the act should include Americans who turned traitor and spied on their own countrymen. On February 27, 1778,

DEATH FOR CAPTURED FOREIGN SPIES

This is the text of the first U.S. espionage act (quoted in the CIA's Intelligence in the War of Independence*).*

Resolved, that all persons not members of, nor owing allegiance to, any of the United States of America, as described in a resolution to the Congress of the 29th of June last, who shall be found lurking as spies in or about the fortification or encampments of the armies of the United States, or of any of them, shall suffer death, according to the law and usage of nations, by sentence of a court martial, or such other punishment as such court martial may direct.

Benjamin Franklin (left) was a member of the original Committee of Secret Correspondence.

therefore, Congress expanded the law to include any "inhabitants of these states"[58] whose intelligence activities gave aid to the enemy.

The passage of the espionage law pleased the commander in chief of the American army, George Washington. More than any other single figure of the period, Washington dominated American intelligence efforts, often personally recruiting spies and dispatching them on their missions. Experience taught him that good intelligence work was vital to the war effort. One of the more disturbing incidents caused by the lack of intelligence occurred in September 1777 when the Americans suffered a defeat at Brandywine, Pennsylvania. In a letter to the president of the Congress, Washington wrote:

Sir: I am sorry to inform you, that in this day's engagement, we have been obliged to leave the enemy masters of the field. Unfortunately the intelligence received of the enemy's advancing up the Brandywine, and crossing at a ford about six miles above us, was uncertain and contradictory, notwithstanding all my pains to get the best. This prevented my making a disposition, adequate to the force with which the enemy attacked us on the right.[59]

Making these words even more bitter was the fact that less than two months before this disaster Washington had made the seminal and now famous statement that would set the tone for the future of American intelligence activities. "The necessity of procuring good intelligence is apparent & need not be further urged," he stated in a letter to one of his officers.

> All that remains for me to add is, that you keep the whole matter as secret as possible. For upon secrecy, success depends in most enterprises of the kind, and for want of it, they are generally defeated, however well planned & promising a favorable issue.[60]

Sending Spies Abroad

To ensure better intelligence collection, Washington and the members of the Committee of Secret Correspondence made every effort to recruit skilled, methodical, and cautious agents. Some of these agents spied in the colonies, while others did so abroad, including in England. The first agent the committee enlisted for foreign work was Arthur Lee, a doctor from Stratford, Connecticut. Franklin and his colleagues sent Lee to England in December 1775, telling him, "It is considered of utmost consequence to the cause of liberty that the Committee be kept informed of developments in Europe."[61] The committee also hired W.F. Dumas, a Swiss journalist working in the Netherlands. Dumas used secret letter drops

Arthur Lee (left) and Silas Deane (below) were two of the first spies employed by the American government in the war.

(depositing letters in prearranged spots) to report back to the committee, as well as to exchange information with Lee in London.

Silas Deane, a former delegate to the Continental Congress, was another important American foreign agent in the war's early years. Disguised as a Bermudian merchant, Deane traveled to France. There, he worked with French merchants to find and recruit French privateers to help disrupt British supply lines. In addition, Deane worked secretly with Lee, and eventually with Franklin himself (when Franklin was appointed a commissioner to France in 1776), to win the French over to the American cause, an effort that eventually succeeded.

Deane also tried to recruit people for sabotage operations against targets in England. The only known such mission that succeeded involved a young American housepainter, James Aitken, who met with Deane in Paris late in 1776. Deane helped Aitken obtain a phony passport, and the two men planned an operation in which Aitken would destroy British shipyards in England using firebombs Aitken himself had designed. An official report issued by the modern Central Intelligence Agency summarizes the results of Aitken's mission:

> In late November 1776, Aitken landed at Dover [on England's southern coast], and on December 7 he ignited a fire at the Portsmouth dockyard that burned from late in the afternoon until the following morning, destroying twenty tons of hemp, ten one-hundred-fathom cables, and six tons of ship cordage.

After failing to penetrate the security at Plymouth, Aitken proceeded to Bristol, where he destroyed two warehouses and several houses. On January 16, 1777, the British cabinet met in emergency session and urged immediate measures to locate the mysterious '*John the Painter.*' . . . Five days later . . . newspapers reported panic throughout England.[62]

Spies in the Former Colonies

At the same time that Aitken was causing damage in England, the committee and General Washington were recruiting spies to infiltrate British-held territories in the former American colonies. Some of these agents disguised themselves as seemingly innocent or harmless individuals. Once behind enemy lines, they gathered information by snooping around sensitive areas or talking to unsuspecting British soldiers or local loyalists.

For example, patriot Robert Townsend pretended to be a merchant, as Silas Deane had. Townsend's cover name, known only to a handful of Americans, including his top boss, Washington, was "Culper, Junior." At a New York coffeehouse frequented by British officers, Townsend often overheard their conversations and duly passed on valuable tidbits of information to another spy, Samuel Woodhull, whose cover name was "Culper, Senior." Woodhull's job was to get the intelligence to General Washington's staff. Scholar John Bakeless, an expert on espionage in the war, outlines the usual careful, roundabout, and effective method employed by the so-called Culper spy ring:

THE CONGRESSIONAL OATH OF SECRECY

American leaders early recognized that it was important to ensure that no intelligence was leaked by any of their number who might be privy to secret information. To guard against this possibility, on November 9, 1775, the Continental Congress adopted an oath of secrecy (quoted in the CIA's Intelligence in the War of Independence) *that read as follows.*

Resolved, that every member of this Congress considers himself under the ties of virtue, honor and love of his country, not to divulge, directly or indirectly, any matter or thing agitated or debated in Congress, before the same shall have been determined, without the leave of the Congress; nor any matter or thing determined in Congress, which a majority of the Congress shall order to be kept secret; and that if any member shall violate this agreement, he shall be expelled from this Congress, and deemed an enemy to the liberties of America, and liable to be treated as such, and that every member signify his consent to this agreement by signing the same.

If Woodhull happened to visit New York when intelligence was ready, Townsend gave it to him orally, to be written down later. . . . Otherwise Townsend turned his reports over to a courier, usually Austin Roe, who made the fifty-mile ride to [the Long Island town where Woodhull lived]. . . . As a precaution, the courier did not visit Woodhull's house, but left the messages in a box, buried in an open field. In due course, Lieutenant Caleb Brewster, a veteran of the whaling trade, crossed Long Island Sound [in a boat] . . . received the reports from Woodhull, and returned to Connecticut, where [American cavalrymen delivered] them to Washington's headquarters.[63]

Among the other American intelligence agents who successfully used disguises and stealth to accomplish their missions was John Honeyman. Sometimes he pretended to be a butcher; other times he posed as a loyalist or an American traitor. He not only collected much valuable information about British military activities in New Jersey but also took part in a crucial deception operation. In December 1776, following Washington's instructions, Honeyman pretended to be an American being hunted for treason. He fell in with the British and Hessians (German mercenaries) in the Trenton area, who believed him when he claimed that Washington's troops were in no shape to fight. This ruse was a major factor in the American victory at Trenton following Washington's surprise crossing of the Delaware River on December 26.

Another successful American agent, Nancy Morgan Hart, was one of several women who spied for the patriots. She took advantage of her unusual physical attributes—Hart was tall, muscular, and

American spy Nancy Moran Hart single-handedly captures a group of loyalists who broke into her home. They were later executed.

cross-eyed—by assuming the identity of a mentally ill homeless man. Managing to penetrate the British lines in Augusta, Georgia, she gained valuable information about the enemy defenses there. Hart was tough, even by male standards. When some loyalists found out she was a spy and attacked her home, she captured them all, handed them over to the patriots, and witnessed their execution.

The Cutting Edge of Danger

The missions described above were all successful. But several others ended in failure, and agents risked capture and death at all times. Indeed, the British were as skilled in ferreting out spies in their midst as the Americans were. One American agent, John

L. Mersereau, the son of one of Washington's officers, had a series of hair-raising escapes, including one that took place on Staten Island in 1778. Mersereau later recalled the incident:

[I] sometimes carried intelligence to the Jersey shore in person. At one time . . . I repaired in the night an old skiff which lay among the grass on a part of the island not then guarded by the British and passed over [to the mainland]. . . . When my business was concluded it was too late to return that night, and I remained on the Jersey side the next day, concealed in a barn. During my absence, the British had noticed the absence of the old skiff and placed a sentry near the place where I had embarked. . . . I landed there without knowing the place was guarded. The sentry hailed, and I fled on my hands and feet to a ditch, along which I could run without being much exposed to his fire. He fired his musket just as I got into the ditch, and his ball struck a post just over my head. I then jumped out of the ditch and ran directly to my lodgings. The sentinel, with others, pursued me [but they were unable to capture me].[64]

Mersereau was lucky to escape in one piece. However, others were not as fortu-nate, among them James Aitken, the American saboteur who had successfully burned docks and warehouses in southern England. Constantly on the run from British authorities, Aitken was eventually apprehended with some of his bomb-making materials still on his person. He refused to admit that he was behind the sabotage, but the British soon managed to find his forged passport and other damn-ing evidence. On March 10, 1777, they hanged Aitken at Portsmouth dockyard, the scene of his first "crime."

Unarguably the most renowned case of an American spy's capture and execu-tion was that of Nathan Hale, a captain in the Connecticut militia. In 1776 Hale

Nathan Hale, the most famous American spy in the war, is about to be hanged by the British.

responded to General Washington's request for a volunteer to gather information in British-held New York. Unfortunately, as spies go Hale was a rank amateur, having no training or experience, no undercover contacts in New York, and no way to communicate with his American superiors. He was captured and hanged before he could make it back with the intelligence he had collected.

In a strange twist of fate, Nathan Hale, the least successful of all the American spies in the war, became the most celebrated of their number, mainly because of the defiant last words attributed to him. "My station was near the fatal spot," remembered Captain William Hull of Connecticut, who witnessed the execution on September 26, 1776,

> and I requested the Provost Marshal to permit the prisoner to sit [with me] while he was making the necessary preparations. Captain Hale entered. He was calm, and bore himself with gentle dignity. . . . He was shortly after summoned to the gallows. [Only] a few persons were around him, yet his characteristic dying words were remembered. He said, "I only regret that I have but one life to lose for my country."[65]

The Most Dangerous Game of All

General Washington had realized the risks of sending an amateur like Nathan Hale to gather intelligence but evidently thought the chances of success outweighed those risks. By contrast, Washington would never have

allowed someone so inexperienced to get involved in the most dangerous spy game of all—counterintelligence. This is the domain of the double agent, someone who pretends to spy for one side but is really spying for the other. To be successful, such an agent must be able to both fool many people and secretly transmit information for extended periods, work requiring exceptional skill and attention to detail.

Perhaps the most successful American double agent of the American Revolution was Enoch Crosby, a veteran soldier in Washington's army. In August 1776 Crosby managed to gain the confidence of a New York loyalist, who believed he shared his views. This allowed Crosby to infiltrate a secret loyalist military company aiding the British against the Americans. He reported the whereabouts of the group's next meeting to the patriots, who captured the loyalists, including Crosby (to maintain his cover). He then "escaped" and returned to his loyalist "friends" and soon afterward joined another loyalist military unit. Thanks to Crosby, this group met the same fate as the first one. The daring double agent repeated the same kind of operation at least four times before the loyalists began to grow suspicious of him.

The intrigues of double agents worked both ways, of course. And General Washington was duly concerned about British spies who might have infiltrated American circles or American traitors working undercover for the British. "There is one evil I dread, and that is, their spies,"[66] Washington told some aides in March 1776.

This fear of the danger posed by enemy spies and American traitors was validated with a vengeance when one of the

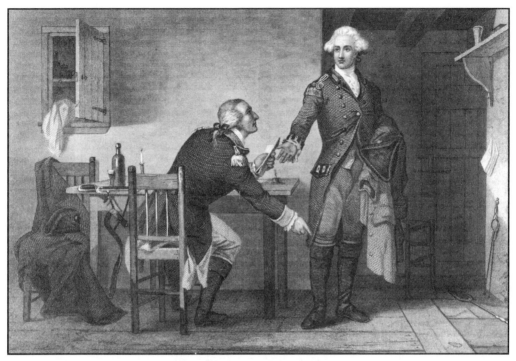

Benedict Arnold, who eventually betrayed his country and went over to the British side, convinces British agent John André to carry his messages to the British camp.

most accomplished American generals, Benedict Arnold, began working with the British in 1780. Arnold was bitter over what he deemed unfair treatment by his superiors; he was also deeply in debt and needed money. So he began hatching secret plans with the British to betray West Point, a post he commanded. Luckily for the Americans, the plot was revealed when Major John André, a British agent who transmitted Arnold's messages, was caught in the act. His cover blown, Arnold fled to the enemy's ranks, where he became a British general. This left André to face the consequences. American intelligence expert Benjamin Tallmadge later recalled escorting André to his trial:

Major André was very inquisitive to know my opinion as to the result of his capture. . . . I said to him that I had a much loved classmate in Yale College by the name of Nathan Hale, who entered the army with me in the year 1776. After the British troops had entered New York . . . Captain Hale tendered his services, went into New York, and was taken just as he was passing the outposts of the enemy. Said I, with emphasis, "Do you remember the sequel to this story?" "Yes," said André. "He was hanged as a spy, but you surely do not consider his case and mine alike." I replied, "Precisely similar will be your fate."[7]

On October 2, 1780, just as Tallmadge had predicted, André met the same fate as Nathan Hale—death by hanging.

Codes and Invisible Inks

If Arnold's message had been somehow unreadable or undecipherable, West Point might have fallen and Major André might not have been hanged. The reality was that many other secret messages passed during the war were rendered unreadable by various methods. For example, American spy Silas Deane used an invisible ink made from cobalt chloride, glycerin, and water. Even more effective was the so-called sympathetic stain invented by James Jay, a doctor and brother of the famous patriot John Jay. The stain consisted of one chemical for writing a message, which quickly became undetectable to the eye, and another chemical that, when applied to the paper, revealed the message. General Washington promoted the use of the stain, saying that it would render a spy's "communications less exposed to detection, but relieve the fears of such persons as may be entrusted in its conveyance."[68]

Eventually, the British captured some papers revealing that the Americans in the New York area were using sympathetic stain. Realizing that some other way to hide information from the enemy had to be found, Benjamin Tallmadge, who often oversaw the members of the Culper spy ring, devised an effective numerical substitution code. According to the CIA's report:

Having been charged as a spy, Major John André receives news that he has been found guilty and sentenced to death. The Americans hanged André in October 1780.

Benjamin Tallmadge, an American soldier and politician, was one of the leaders of the Culper spy ring.

Tallmadge took several hundred words from a dictionary and several dozen names of people or places and assigned each a number from 1 to 763. For example, 38 meant attack, 192 stood for fort, George Washington was identified as 711, and New York was replaced by 727. An American agent posing as a deliveryman transmitted the messages to other members of the ring. One of them, Anna Strong, signaled the messages' location with a code involving laundry hung out to dry. A black petticoat indicated that a message was ready to be picked up.[69]

Methods of secret writing, as well as other espionage practices developed during the American Revolution, helped the patriots win the war. They also laid the foundation of the U.S. intelligence community, which has played a crucial role in most of the wars the country has fought since that time. As Washington so shrewdly pointed out, victory in war almost always requires reliable intelligence, which time and again has proved itself to be just as crucial as guns, bombs, and warships.

Notes

Introduction: How the Patriots Beat the Odds and Won

1. Quoted in William Dudley, ed., *The American Revolution: Opposing Viewpoints,* Greenhaven Press, 1992, pp. 154–55.
2. Ian V. Hogg, *Armies of the American Revolution*. Englewood Cliffs, NJ: Prentice Hall, 1975, p. 16.
3. Henry S. Commager and Richard B. Morris, eds., *The Spirit of 'Seventy-Six: The Story of the American Revolution as Told by Participants*, 2 vols. New York: Bobbs-Merrill, 1958, vol. 1, pp. 89–90.
4. Samuel E. Morison, *The Oxford History of the American People*. New York: Oxford University Press, 1965, pp. 237–38.
5. Quoted in G.D. Scull, ed., *Memoir and Letters of Captain W. Glanville Evelyn, of the Fourth Regiment from North America, 1774–1776*. Oxford, England: James Parker, 1879, pp. 53–55.
6. Quoted in Clarence E. Carter, ed., *The Correspondence of General Thomas Gage*. 2 vols. New Haven, CT: Yale University Press, 1931–1932, vol. 2, pp. 686–87.

Chapter 1: Making and Operating Handheld Guns

7. Archer Jones, *The Art of War in the Western World*. New York: Oxford University Press, 1987, pp. 269–70.
8. Hogg, *Armies of the Revolution*, p. 64.
9. Quoted in Hogg, *Armies of the Revolution*, pp. 45–46.
10. Frederick von Steuben, *Baron von Steuben's Revolutionary War Drill Manual*. Mineola, NY: Dover, 1985, pp. 99–100.
11. Hogg, *Armies of the Revolution*, p. 66.
12. Quoted in Morison, *Oxford History of the American People*, p. 232.
13. Quoted in Jeremy Black, *Warfare in the Eighteenth Century*. London: Cassell, 1999, p. 118.
14. George Hanger, *Colonel George Hanger to All Sportsmen*. London: J.J. Stockdale, 1814, pp. 207–10.

15. Quoted in Hugh F. Rankin, ed., *The American Revolution*. New York: G.P. Putnam's Sons, 1964, p. 263.

16. Warren Moore, *Weapons of the American Revolution and Accouterments*. New York: Promontory Press, 1967, pp. 7–8.

Chapter 2: Many Traditional Bladed Weapons

17. George C. Neumann, *Swords and Blades of the American Revolution*. Harrisburg, PA: Stackpole Books, 1973, pp. 22–23.

18. Quoted in Henry P. Johnston, *The Storming of Stony Point on the Hudson, Midnight, July 15, 1779: Its Importance in the Light of Unpublished Documents*. New York: J.T. White, 1900, pp. 174–75.

19. Epaphras Hoyt, *Treatise on the Military Art*. Brattleborough, VT: Smead, 1798, p. 101.

20. Quoted in John C. Dann, ed., *The Revolution Remembered: Eyewitness Accounts of the War for Independence*. Chicago: University of Chicago Press, 1980, p. 275.

21. Quoted in John C. Fitzpatrick, ed., *The Writings of George Washington*, 39 vols. Washington, DC: U.S. Government Printing House, 1933–1944, vol. 10, p. 190.

22. Quoted in Fitzpatrick, *Writings of George Washington*, vol. 8, p. 236.

23. Quoted in Harold L. Peterson, *Arms and Armor in Colonial America*. Mineola, NY: Dover, 2000, p. 294.

Chapter 3: Battle Tactics Old and New

24. Black, *Warfare in the Eighteenth Century*, p. 112.

25. Quoted in Commager and Morris, *Spirit of 'Seventy-Six*, vol. 1, pp. 577–78.

26. Quoted in Black, *Warfare in the Eighteenth Century*, p. 114.

27. Quoted in Black, *Warfare in the Eighteenth Century*, p. 118.

28. Quoted in Rankin, *American Revolution*, p. 261.

29. Neumann, *Swords and Blades*, pp. 18–19.

30. Quoted in Commager and Morris, *Spirit of 'Seventy-Six*, vol. 1, pp. 127–28.

31. Quoted in Dann, *The Revolution Remembered*, pp. 194–95.

32. Quoted in Henry Onderdonk, *Revolutionary Incidents of Suffolk and King's Counties: With an Account of the Battle of Long Island and the British Prisons and Prison-Ships at New York*. New York: Leavitt, 1849, pp. 147–48.

33. Quoted in Kenneth Roberts, *The Battle of Cowpens: The Story of 900 Men Who Shook an Empire*. Garden City, NY: Doubleday, 1958, p. 87.

34. James Collins, *Autobiography of a Revolutionary Soldier*, ed. John M. Roberts. Clinton, LA: Feliciana Democrat, 1859, pp. 264–65.

Chapter 4: The Urgent Need for Cannons

35. Hogg, *Armies of the Revolution*, p. 131.

36. Hogg, *Armies of the Revolution*, p. 132.

37. John Muller, *A Treatise on Artillery*. 1756; reprint, Ottawa, Canada: Museum Restoration Service, 1965, p. 58.

38. H.C.B. Rogers, *A History of Artillery*. Secaucus, NJ: Citadel Press, 1975, pp. 171–72.

39. Albert Manucy, *Artillery Through the Ages: A Short Illustrated History of Cannon, Emphasizing Types Used in America*. Washington, DC: U.S. Government Printing Office, 1949, p. 11.

40. Quoted in Robert S. Quimby, *The Background of Napoleonic Warfare: The Theory of Military Tactics in Eighteenth-Century France*. New York: AMS Press, 1968, p. 296.

41. Quoted in Jones, *Art of War*, pp. 298–99.

42. Joseph P. Martin, *Private Yankee Doodle: Being a Narrative of Some of the Adventures, Dangers, and Sufferings of a Revolutionary Soldier*. 1830; reprint, ed. George E. Scheer, Boston: Little, Brown, 1962, pp. 96–97.

43. Quoted in Dann, *The Revolution Remembered*, pp. 239–40.

44. James Thacher, *A Military Journal During the American Revolutionary War, from 1775–1783, Describing Interesting Events and Transactions of This Period*. Boston: Cottons and Barnard, 1827, pp. 283–84.

45. Quoted in Black, *Warfare in the Eighteenth Century*, p. 124.

Chapter 5: David Versus Goliath on the High Seas

46. Commager and Morris, *Spirit of 'Seventy-Six*, vol. 2, p. 912.

47. Jack Coggins, *Ships and Seamen of the American Revolution*. Harrisburg, PA: Stackpole Books, 1969, p. 21.

48. Coggins, *Ships and Seamen*, p. 21.

49. Quoted in Charles F. Adams, ed., *The Works of John Adams, Second President of the United States: With a Life of the Author, Notes, and Illustrations*, 10 vols. Boston: Little, Brown, 1850–1856, vol. 3, p. 8.

50. Quoted in Gardner W. Allen, *A Naval History of the American Revolution*, 2 vols. Gansevoort, NY: Corner House, 1970, vol. 1, p. 60.

51. *Rules for the Regulation of the Navy of the United Colonies of North-America*. 1775; reprint, Washington, DC: Naval Historical Foundation, 1944, p. 3.

52. Coggins, *Ships and Seamen*, pp. 149–50.

53. Quoted in Allen, *Naval History*, vol. 1, pp. 60–61.

54. Quoted in Commager and Morris, *Spirit of 'Seventy-Six*, vol. 2, pp. 919–20.

55. Quoted in Commager and Morris, *Spirit of 'Seventy-Six*, vol. 2, p. 948.

56. Quoted in Commager and Morris, *Spirit of 'Seventy-Six*, vol. 1, p. 222.

57. Quoted in Commager and Morris, *Spirit of 'Seventy-Six*, vol. 1, p. 220.

Chapter 6: The Secret War: American and British Spies

58. Quoted in Central Intelligence Agency, *Intelligence in the War of Independence*. Washington, DC: Central Intelligence Agency, n.d., p. 4.

59. Quoted in Fitzpatrick, *Writings of George Washington*, vol. 9, p. 207.

60. Quoted in Fitzpatrick, *Writings Of George Washington*, vol. 8, p. 85.

61. Quoted in CIA, *Intelligence*, p. 7.

62. CIA, *Intelligence*, p. 9.

63. John Bakeless, *Turncoats, Traitors, and Heroes: Espionage in the American Revolution*. Philadelphia: Lippincott, 1953, p. 228.

64. Quoted in Dann, *The Revolution Remembered*, pp. 349–50.

65. Quoted in Maria Hull Campbell, *Revolutionary Services and Civil Life of General William Hull; Prepared from His Manuscripts*. New York: D. Appleton, 1848, p. 38.

66. Quoted in CIA, *Intelligence*, pp. 10–11.

67. Quoted in Rankin, *American Revolution*, pp. 208–209.

68. Quoted in CIA, *Intelligence*, p. 15.

69. CIA, *Intelligence*, p. 16.

Glossary

artillery: Cannons; also generally called ordnance.

bore: The inside of a gun's barrel.

breech: The back end of a gun's barrel.

caliber: The specific width of a gun's bore usually expressed in decimal form, in inches.

covert: Undercover.

cutlass: A single-edged sword, somewhat shorter than a saber, that became a standard sailor's weapon by the second half of the eighteenth century.

espionage: Spying or intelligence work.

flank: The side or wing of a military formation. To "outflank" the enemy is to move one's own troops around his flanks, exposing them to attack from the side and rear as well as the front.

flintlock: A mechanism for firing a gun in which a piece of flint strikes a piece of steel, producing a spark that ignites the gunpowder.

frigate: A sail-driven warship equipped with between twenty and forty-four cannons.

grapeshot: A mass of small iron balls fired by a cannon.

grenadier: Originally an infantry soldier who threw grenades at the enemy; by the time of the American Revolution, it referred to an elite infantry soldier who used more conventional weapons.

gun: In terms of artillery, a cannon with a long barrel that fired shot in low trajectories, best suited for use on an open battlefield where targets were in plain sight.

halberd: A long spear with an axlike blade attached at or near the front end.

howitzer: A cannon with a barrel length falling between those of artillery guns and mortars; a howitzer could fire somewhat higher than an artillery gun.

intelligence: In military terms, information about one's enemy accumulated by spying or other means.

linear tactics: The European or Continental tactical system in which opposing lines of soldiers, usually equipped with muskets and bayonets, marched toward each other in the open.

matchlock: A mechanism for firing a gun in which pulling the trigger brings a lighted match into contact with a small pan of gunpowder, which flashes and ignites the gunpowder inside the barrel.

mortar: A cannon with a wide, short barrel designed for firing shells in a high trajectory, usually over fortress or city walls.

musket (or firelock): An early gun with a smooth bore that fired by means of either a matchlock or flintlock mechanism.

muzzle: The front end of a gun's barrel.

ordnance: Artillery or cannons.

pike: A very long spear.

plug bayonet: An early kind of bayonet that was inserted into the barrel of a musket, plugging it and rendering it incapable of firing.

pole arm: Any of a class of weapons featuring a blade attached to a pole, including spears, pikes, halberds, and spontoons.

quoin: A wooden wedge placed under the rear of a cannon to lower the angle of its muzzle.

ramrod: A stick used by early gunmen to push the powder and ball down into the gun barrel.

rifle: A gun with a rifled bore or a barrel that has a set of spiral grooves etched on its inside.

saber: A slashing sword used mainly by cavalrymen.

schooner: A large sailboat.

shell: A metal container filled with gunpowder fired from a cannon.

shot: Solid balls fired from cannons or lead balls or pellets fired from muskets or rifles.

smoothbore: A firearm, such as the musket, that has a barrel with a smooth inside surface.

socket bayonet: A kind of bayonet that attached to the outside of the barrel of a gun so that the weapon could be fired without removing the bayonet.

spontoon: A long spear or short pike, often having a fancy-shaped blade.

tampion: A wooden plug stuffed into the barrel of a naval cannon when not in use to keep out moisture.

windage: In firearms, the space between the edge of the ball (or bullet) and the inside of the barrel.

For Further Reading

Judith E. Harper, *African Americans and the Revolutionary War*. Chanhaussen, MN: Child's World, 2000. A well-written and informative examination of a largely forgotten chapter of the American fight for independence—the role played by black patriots.

Deborah Kent, *Lexington and Concord*. Danbury, CT: Childrens Press, 1997. Aimed at young readers, this is an excellent overview of the opening battles of the American Revolution.

Stuart Murray, *Eyewitness: The American Revolution*. London: Dorling Kindersley, 2002. A beautifully illustrated volume that covers vitually all the major aspects of the war. Highly recommended.

Don Nardo, *Opposing Viewpoints Digests: The American Revolution*. San Diego: Greenhaven Press, 1998. A collection of extensively documented essays containing a wide range of opinions and debates about the conflict between Britain and its American colonies.

Diane Smolinski, *Land Battles of the Revolutionary War*. Crystal Lake, IL: Heinemann Library, 2001. A fine overview of the major land battles fought in the war, including Trenton, Cowpens, and Yorktown.

———, *Revolutionary War Soldiers*. Crystal Lake, IL: Heinemann Library, 2001. Another excellent book about the Revolutionary War by Smolinski; this one covers the enlistment, weapons, uniforms, training, and duties of the soldiers who fought in the war.

Linda R. Wade, *Early Battles of the American Revolution*. Edina, MN: Abdo, 2001. An effective synopsis of the initial engagements fought in the American war for independence.

Marko Zlatich, *General Washington's Army. 1775–1778* and *1779–1783*. Oxford: Osprey, 1994–1995. Two handsomely illustrated books showing full-color reconstructions of the uniforms and weapons used by the American soldiers during the Revolution. Highly recommended.

Major Works Consulted

Primary Sources

Charles F. Adams, ed., *The Works of John Adams, Second President of the United States: With a Life of the Author, Notes, and Illustrations*, 10 vols. Boston: Little, Brown, 1850–1856.

Humphrey Bland, *A Treatise on Military Discipline*. New York: Hugh Gaine, 1759.

Maria Hull Campbell, *Revolutionary Services and Civil Life of General William Hull; Prepared from His Manuscripts*. New York: D. Appleton, 1848.

Clarence E. Carter, ed., *The Correspondence of General Thomas Gage*, 2 vols. New Haven, CT: Yale University Press, 1931–1932.

Central Intelligence Agency, *Intelligence in the War of Independence*. Washington, DC: Central Intelligence Agency, n.d.

James Collins, *Autobiography of a Revolutionary Soldier*. Ed. John M. Roberts. Clinton, LA: Feliciana Democrat, 1859.

Henry S. Commager and Richard B. Morris, eds., *The Spirit of 'Seventy-Six: The Story of the American Revolution as Told by Participants*, 2 vols. New York: Bobbs-Merrill, 1958.

John C. Dann, ed., *The Revolution Remembered: Eyewitness Accounts of the War for Independence*. Chicago: University of Chicago Press, 1980.

William Dudley, ed., *The American Revolution: Opposing Viewpoints*. San Diego: Greenhaven Press, 1992.

John C. Fitzpatrick, ed., *The Writings of George Washington*, 39 vols. Washington, DC: U.S. Government Printing House, 1933–1944.

George Hanger, *Colonel George Hanger to All Sportsmen*. London: J.J. Stockdale, 1814.

Epaphras Hoyt, *Treatise on the Military Art*. Brattleborough, VT: Smead, 1798.

Charles Hudson, *History of the Town of Lexington, Middlesex County, Massachusetts, from Its First Settlement to 1868*. Boston: Houghton Mifflin, 1913.

Henry P. Johnston, *The Storming of Stony Point on the Hudson, Midnight, July 15, 1779: Its Importance in the Light of Unpublished Documents.* New York: J.T. White, 1900.

Joseph P. Martin, *Private Yankee Doodle: Being a Narrative of Some of the Adventures, Dangers, and Sufferings of a Revolutionary Soldier.* 1830; reprint, ed. George E. Scheer, Boston: Little, Brown, 1962.

Samuel E. Morison, ed., *Sources and Documents Illustrating the American Revolution, 1764–1788, and the Formation of the Federal Constitution.* Oxford, England: Clarendon Press, 1953.

Richard B. Morris, ed., *The American Revolution, 1763–1783: A Bicentennial Collection.* Columbia: University of South Carolina Press, 1970.

John Muller, *A Treatise on Artillery.* 1756; reprint, Ottawa, Canada: Museum Restoration Service, 1965.

Henry Onderdonk, *Revolutionary Incidents of Suffolk and King's Counties: With an Account of the Battle of Long Island and the British Prisons and Prison-Ships at New York.* New York: Leavitt, 1849.

Howard H. Peckham, ed., *Sources of American Independence*, 2 vols. Chicago: University of Chicago Press, 1978.

Hugh F. Rankin, ed., *The American Revolution.* New York: G.P. Putnam's Sons, 1964.

Rhode Island Records, 1772–1777. State archives, Providence, RI. *Rules for the Regulation of the Navy of the United Colonies of North-America.* 1775; reprint, Washington DC: Naval Historical Foundation, 1944.

G.D. Scull, ed., *Memoir and Letters of Captain W. Glanville Evelyn, of the Fourth Regiment from North America, 1774–1776.* Oxford, England: James Parker, 1879.

Frederick von Steuben, *Baron von Steuben's Revolutionary War Drill Manual.* Mineola, NY: Dover, 1985.

James Thacher, *A Military Journal During the American Revolutionary War, from 1775–1783, Describing Interesting Events and Transactions of This Period.* Boston: Cottons and Barnard, 1827.

Modern Sources

Gardner W. Allen, *A Naval History of the American Revolution*, 2 vols. Gansevoort, NY: Corner House, 1970. A large, detailed study of the naval engagements of the war.

John Bakeless, *Turncoats, Traitors, and Heroes: Espionage in the American Revolution.* Philadelphia: Lippincott, 1953. One of the two classic modern studies of espionage during the war for independence. (The other is Carl van Doren's book; see below.) This is an information-packed, absorbing read.

Jeremy Black, *Warfare in the Eighteenth Century.* London: Cassell, 1999. A handy general overview of the weapons, tactics, and military advancements of the century in which the American Revolution took place.

Charles K. Bolton, *The Private Soldier Under Washington.* Gansevoort, NY:

Corner House, 1997. Perhaps the best general study of the average American soldier in the war for independence, including information about recruitment, camps, weapons, training, and more.

Jack Coggins, *Ships and Seamen of the American Revolution*. Harrisburg, PA: Stackpole Books, 1969. An excellent synopsis of the warships and sailors that fought in the war, including data on shipbuilding, weapons, experiments with submarines, and descriptions of major battles.

Edward Countryman, *The American Revolution*. New York: Hill and Wang, 1985. Arguably the most authoritative single-volume general history of the American war for independence, this is a large, richly documented, and engrossing study. Highly recommended.

Robert A. Gross, *The Minutemen and Their World*. New York: Hill and Wang, 1976. A well-written, well-documented summary of the men who fought in the colonial and later state militia during the American Revolution.

Ian V. Hogg, *Armies of the American Revolution*. Englewood Cliffs, NJ: Prentice Hall, 1975. This excellent overview of the military aspects of the war contains numerous color illustrations.

Archer Jones, *The Art of War in the Western World*. New York: Oxford University Press, 1987. An excellent academic, though nonscholarly treatment of the history of Western warfare by a respected military historian. Jones devotes a long, well-organized chapter to the infantry tactics of the eighteenth century, which characterized much of the fighting in the American Revolution.

Robin May, *The British Army in North America, 1775–1783*. Oxford, England: Osprey, 1997. A fine, beautifully illustrated overview of British troops during the American Revolution, focusing mainly on their units and uniforms, but also including information on recruitment and pay.

Warren Moore, *Weapons of the American Revolution and Accouterments*. New York: Promontory Press, 1967. One of the better general synopses of the handheld weapons of the war and the accessories carried by their users.

George C. Neumann, *Swords and Blades of the American Revolution*. Harrisburg, PA: Stackpole Books, 1973. A very clearly written and informational study of the bayonets, swords, daggers, axes, halberds, and spears used in the conflict. Highly recommended.

Carl van Doren, *Secret History of the American Revolution*. Clifton, NJ: Augustus M. Kelley, 1973. A fulsome telling of the spies, traitors, and other individuals who gathered intelligence for both sides in the war.

W.J. Wood, *Battles of the Revolutionary War, 1775–1781*. New York: Da Capo Press, 1995. This is one of the better general overviews of the major battles fought in the conflict.

Additional Works Consulted

David F. Butler, *United States Firearms: The First Century, 1776–1875*. New York: Winchester Press, 1971.

Martha Byrd, *Saratoga: Turning Point of the American Revolution*. Philadelphia: Auerbach, 1973.

Philip Davidson, *Propaganda and the American Revolution, 1763–1783*. New York: W.W. Norton, 1973.

Thomas Flexner, *George Washington*. Boston: Little, Brown, 1968.

Albert N. Hardin Jr., *The American Bayonet, 1776–1964*. Philadelphia: Riling and Lentz, 1964.

B.P. Hughes, *British Smooth Bore Artillery: The Muzzle-Loading Artillery of the 18th and 19th Centuries*. Harrisburg, PA: Stackpole, 1969.

Pauline Maier, *From Resistance to Revolution*. New York: Knopf, 1972.

Albert Manucy, *Artillery Through the Ages: A Short Illustrated History of Cannon, Emphasizing Types Used in America*. Washington, DC: U.S. Government Printing Office, 1949.

Samuel E. Morison, *The Oxford History of the American People*. New York: Oxford University Press, 1965.

Harold L. Peterson, *Arms and Armor in Colonial America*. Mineola, NY: Dover, 2000.

———, *The Treasury of the Gun*. New York: Golden Press, 1962.

Robert S. Quimby, *The Background of Napoleonic Warfare: The Theory of Military Tactics in Eighteenth-Century France*. New York: AMS Press, 1968.

Stuart Reid, *British Redcoat, 1740–1793*. Oxford, England: Osprey, 1996.

Kenneth Roberts, *The Battle of Cowpens: The Story of 900 Men Who Shook an Empire*. Garden City, NY: Doubleday, 1958.

H.C.B. Rogers, *A History of Artillery*. Secaucus, NJ: Citadel Press, 1975.

———, *The Mounted Troops of the British Army*. London: Seeley, 1959.

———, *Weapons of the British Soldier*. London: Seeley, 1960.

John Shy, *A People Numerous and Armed: Reflections on the Military Struggle* for *American Independence*. New York: Oxford University Press, 1976.

——, *Toward Lexington: The Role of the British Army in the Coming of the American Revolution*. Princeton, NJ: Princeton University Press, 1965.

Robert W. Tucker and David C. Hendrickson, *The Fall of the First British Empire*. Baltimore, MD; Johns Hopkins University Press, 1982.

Irwin Unger, *These United States: The Questions of Our Past*. Vol. 1. Boston: Little, Brown, 1978.

Howard Zinn, *A People's History of the United States*. New York: HarperCollins, 1980.

Index

Picture Credits

Cover Photo: Bridgeman Art Library
Art Archive, 65
Art Archive/Gunshots, 26, 30
© Bettmann/CORBIS, 38, 84
© Christie's Images/CORBIS, 36
© CORBIS, 81
Dover Publications, 23, 59
© John Heseltine/CORBIS, 73
© Hulton/Archive by Getty Images, 14, 16, 17, 18, 49, 57, 60, 63, 80, 85, 87, 88, 89
Library of Congress, 45

© The Mariner's Museum/CORBIS, 73
Mary Evans Picture Library, 29, 76
North Wind Picture Archives, 12, 20, 25, 32, 41, 43, 47, 62, 64, 68, 74, 75, 81
© Richard T. Nowitz/CORBIS, 31
© Carl and Ann Purcell/CORBIS, 56
© Sohm; ChromoSohm, Inc./CORBIS, 55
© Paul A. Souders/CORBIS, 70
© Ted Speigel/CORBIS, 34
Stock Montage, Inc., 42

About the Author

Historian Don Nardo has written many books for young adults about American wars, among them *The Mexican-American War*, *The War of 1812*, *World War II in the Pacific*, and volumes on the weapons and tactics of the Indian Wars and Civil War. Mr. Nardo lives with his wife, Christine, in Massachusetts.